Henry Loomis Nelson

The money we need

a short primer on money and currency

Henry Loomis Nelson

The money we need
a short primer on money and currency

ISBN/EAN: 9783337414542

Printed in Europe, USA, Canada, Australia, Japan

Cover: Foto ©Suzi / pixelio.de

More available books at **www.hansebooks.com**

THE MONEY WE NEED

A SHORT PRIMER
ON
MONEY AND CURRENCY

BY

HENRY LOOMIS NELSON

The good money that we have is enough
Any cheap money is too much

NEW YORK
HARPER & BROTHERS PUBLISHERS
1895

NOTE

THE diagrams accompanying the paper on "The Money We Need" were prepared by Mr. WORTHINGTON C. FORD, Chief of the Bureau of Statistics, at Washington, and for this and other kind assistance I desire to thank him and the Hon. JOHN DEWITT WARNER.

H. L. N.

CONTENTS

ILLUSTRATIONS

THE MONEY WE NEED

I

THE subject of money and the laws which govern
its distribution have been made to appear so complicated that not only persons of ordinary intelligence,
but experts on other subjects, shrink from an article
or a book on money on account of its presumed in-
comprehensibility. A strange mystery has grown up
in connection with a subject that concerns every civilized human being, and this mystery has been det-
rimental to the interests of commerce in goods and
services. The ills that come to merchants, manufacturers, and working-men—to all who have anything
to sell or any desire to buy—have been increased and
complicated by the money question as it has been
presented in different phases at different periods by
theorists, speculators, and the unthrifty. It has served
the purpose of some persons at crucial periods to
practise deception concerning the nature of money.
It has been in the past and still is believed that
money could be made out of anything by the fiat
of the government. Some people have professed to
think that much money in a country means general
prosperity, and they point to the time of the war of

secession and to the greenbacks of our own country, to the period when the nation was piling up an enormous war debt, which the people have since been paying off through burdensome taxes. They think that because some manufacturers of shoddy, some sutlers, and some contractors made their fortunes in those days, the whole country grew rich, and that it was the cheap greenbacks that blessed us. Many persons who are ready to permit others to do their thinking for them accept this as the truth; and yet if they stop to think for themselves, their reason will tell them that a country cannot grow rich by maintaining great armies. Riches are not gained in this way by those who stay at home and pay out of their earnings for the food, the shelter, the clothing, the weapons, the powder and bullets, the medical care, and for the transportation of the thousands of soldiers in the field. It will tell them also that the wealth of a country consists in what it produces; and therefore if a hundred thousand citizens are taken from the fields and the shops to fight their neighbors, the aggregate production for the time during which they are engaged in international or domestic murder will be less than it is when they are employed in the less glorious arts of peace, and therefore the wealth of the nation will be less. A nation cannot grow rich by fighting unless it conquers the enemy, and compels him to pay not only the expenses of the war, but a handsome profit on them. But up to this time no nation that ever succeeded in a war has received back anything like its awful cost. There is no reason to believe that any conqueror will ever be repaid in wealth or its representative, money, for the expenditure which he is forced to incur to win his triumph. Reason will also tell our easy-going friends that no country can get rich by printing pieces of paper and calling them dollars.

And yet the assertion that the United States grew rich during the war by making trade for the shoddy-mills and the sutlers is quite as worthy of respect as many of the arguments which are addressed to Congress and the country by those who are in favor of the silver dollar instead of the gold dollar, or of bimetallism, which means the same thing as a single silver standard, or of paper dollars printed by the government in quantities to suit. Whatever is said here must not be considered as addressed personally to all who believe that something radical ought to be done to reform our money system. A good many honest people have been deceived, and a good many intelligent people have been mystified, by the speculations of those for whose apparently studious pursuit of this subject they have respect. They have been led to believe, for example, that there is not enough gold in the world for the proper transaction of the world's business; that gold has increased in value, become dearer, and that therefore it pur-

chases more of other products than it used to. There
is a universal outcry about low prices, and sugges-
tions are made that if silver were used for money as
well as gold, money would be cheaper and other
products would be dearer. The idea has gained
ground that money is something valuable in itself,
something that men, especially bankers, pursue for
its own sake, because they want to store it up.
Therefore these greedy persons have devised methods, arts, tricks—all of them dishonorable and tyran-
nical—by the practice of which they may gather in
the money of the world and compel others who
want it to pay enormously for it.

It seems to me, now that Congress has adjourned
—the one Congress of all the legislative bodies that
ever met in Washington which did most to becloud
this question—that it is well to make an attempt to
think back out of the maze with which the philoso-
phers have surrounded money, currency, and banking
to the simple principles that underlie the subject.

II

WHAT is wealth? What is money? These are
the questions which first present themselves. The
political economists find great difficulty in defining
wealth, but for our purposes we may say that every
material thing which man may use or enjoy, and
which may be bought and sold, is wealth. Corn,
cloth, houses, carriages and horses, and the works
of art and literature — all these constitute wealth.
Money is the tool by which wealth is exchanged. It
is only a tool or a vehicle. For itself merely it is
not desirable. It is only desirable because it enables
A to exchange what he has for something that he
desires without going through the clumsy, sometimes
the impossible, process of a barter.

Money is a vehicle. It carries exchanges. It has
also been likened to a tool, because men transact
business with it. Melted down it may be sold by
weight, as coffee, tea, or sugar is sold. Men collect
coins, it is true. Some coins are artistic, while
others have historical or antiquarian interest; but a
sovereign or a dollar, considered as money, has
merely the power of purchasing articles which men

need or enjoy. A man might possess a bank full of money, but he would go hungry or naked for all that if there were no food or raiment for him to buy.

Money was invented for men's convenience. All great economic truth is essentially the same where-ever it is applied. The same laws govern the small trading of the simplest community and the large and complicated transactions of countries like the United States, Great Britain, France, and Germany. The great fundamental truth about money is that it must not be doubted. A coined piece should have a definite value, a universally recognized signifi-cance. When it does not mean the same thing to the man who sells as to the man who buys, it ceases to be able to perform its function perfectly. In a small community there is a man who grows wheat, another who rises sheep and clips them for their wool, one who is a butcher, one who makes cloth, one who is a tailor. If barter prevailed, the farmer, when he wanted a coat, would be obliged to carry his wheat, after it was grown, to the tailor, and ex-change it for a coat. A good deal of time and labor would be wasted in this process. But if the tailor happened to be supplied with all the wheat that he wanted, the farmer would be in a still more uncom-fortable plight. He would be obliged to carry his wheat from one neighbor to another, until he found one who wanted his wheat, and who had something to give in exchange which the tailor wanted. Then he could procure his coat. Money does away with all this trouble. It facilitates exchange. With money in his purse, the farmer would give the tailor the price that he demanded, and the tailor would accept the money because he would know that at any time it would procure for him, in whatever products he might desire, the worth of the coat which he had sold to the farmer. This is the first essential of money, that the man who receives it for what he has to sell shall know that it will always and anywhere procure for him just as much value as that with which he has parted. In a community where all the people know and trust one another almost anything might pass for money. But when any member of such a community wanted to buy something in a neighboring village where he was not known, he would be obliged to offer his products in exchange, or money in which the person of whom he wished to buy had confidence.

This is why money must have intrinsic value. There are various kinds of money or currency, money and currency being confused along with other things that go to make up the mystery of finance. Money is coined metal, and it is necessary that it shall be composed of material that is valuable in itself; that is, which can be melted down and sold for other coin or products for very nearly the sum which is expressed on its face, and that its value shall be stable. As it is the instrument with which exchanges are carried on, it is a standard of value. It is that in which the farmer expresses the worth of his wheat, and the tailor expresses the worth of his coat. Some modern writers on finance, whose books are circulating just now in various parts of this country, are denying this attribute to money. But this is one of the paths by which men wander away from clear reasoning into the haze of the "currency question." It is sufficient for the mind that is trying to get at the truth to remember that we say in our common speech that a bushel of wheat is worth a certain part of a dollar; that it used to be worth a full dollar; that a house or a horse is worth so many dollars; and that we can gratify our desire for any article of merchandise only by giving for it as many dollars as its owner believes will enable him, in turn, to procure something of equal value that he desires. Therefore it is essential that the significance of a dollar should be definite and certain. Moreover, there cannot be dollars or sovereigns made from two metals that not only differ in value, but one of which is frequently changing in value, so that no fixed relationship can be established between the two.

Suppose, for example, in the simple community which we have imagined, that a dollar in gold was intrinsically worth 100 cents, and that the dollar in silver was worth 50 cents, both being legal tenders,

THE SILVER DOLLAR UNDISGUISED

would the farmer like to sell a gold dollar's worth of wheat for a silver dollar? Would he not know that his wheat would thereby be worth less in coats or groceries, or any other commodities that he might need? But the tailor would pay him in silver, and he, in turn, would pay the person whom he owed in the cheap metal. The gold would be hoarded and sent to the neighboring village where it was respected, while the people of this neighboring village would scrape together all the silver they could find in order to pay with it their debts to those who accepted silver as current money. The consequence is that silver would grow cheaper and cheaper, it would buy less and less; finally the neighbors of those who employed it as money would cease to trust them, the payment of debts would be demanded, the sheriff would be busy with foreclosure sales, and commerce and trade would decline.

Money must be honest. The business of the world depends upon the general recognition that money tells the truth on its face. And gold alone receives that general recognition. Even silver countries prefer to receive gold. Some Silver Senators insist in their contracts that they shall be paid in gold. It does not matter what ought to be thought of silver; gold is the only metal in which there is universal confidence.

III

METAL money is the basic money. There are also representatives of money, for money has its representatives, its agents that do its work for it, just as money itself does the work for those who want to trade off the goods they have for goods that others have. Metal money is often inconvenient. It is too heavy, for one thing, to be used in large quantities. When this is true it is open to all the objections that are made against barter. It will not serve for currency in some transactions. By currency, I mean money and its representatives that pass from hand to hand in daily transactions. Suppose, for example, that A should purchase property of B for $100,000. If A had nothing but gold in which to pay B, he would be obliged to buy a wagon and carry the price to B in this expensive and troublesome manner. If there were nothing but gold in the world, the man who goes into the central part of New York State to buy butter and cheese, or to the wheat farms of the Northwest, would be obliged to carry with him chests of gold and an arsenal for his protection against robbers. Therefore paper currency and other representatives of money have been invented. And this paper is not confined to government notes and bank-notes. It does not necessarily represent gold or silver, but it must be good for every dollar that it promises to pay, and, more than that, it must be believed to be good by those who are asked to part with their goods for it. It includes promissory notes, drafts, bills of exchange, and the checks of individuals. All these things pass from hand to hand, and the paper obligations of private persons, it is estimated, furnish the tools with which nine-tenths of business transactions are carried on. All these paper obligations rest on coined money or property of some other kind. They pass in trade because it is believed that they will be redeemed. Paper representatives of money must be honest just as money itself must be honest.

I have said that money is for the convenience of men. It not only does away with barter, but it facilitates and hastens trade and commerce. Since money was introduced men have been constantly devising methods to increase its convenience. The best paper currency is that which is issued by banks. It is best because it has a wider circulation, and is therefore more useful and effective than paper resting on the trust or confidence felt in individuals. The safety of the holder of the bank-bill is best secured, of course, by the guarantee of the government. This guarantee of the government may be furnished in various ways. The national bank-note in this country is safe because there are in the hands of the government bonds of the United States, belonging to the banks, amply sufficient for the redemption of every note. The difficulty with this national bank-note circulation is that its amount depends upon the amount of the public debt. The debt of this government has been paid off with a rapidity that is marvellous, so that while the population and exchanges of the country have been increasing, the amount of bank-note circulation has been diminishing.

The national bank-notes have been replaced by government paper representing gold and silver, but principally silver. That people greatly prefer paper to silver is illustrated by the history of the silver certificates and the efforts of the government to force silver dollars into circulation. In 1886, when there had been coined in silver $233,723,286, the amount of silver dollars actually in circulation was $52,668,623. In 1895 the coinage of silver had increased to $423,-289,219, the Treasury held $124,479,849 in uncoined silver, and the amount of silver in circulation had fallen to $51,983,162. At the same time the certificates representing silver dollars had so increased that the amount of silver held in the Treasury for their redemption had increased from $88,116,225 to $371,306,057.

But we are now inquiring what money really is,

what it means, and what laws govern it, and determine its amount and its distribution. Paper currency issued by banks, its origin and operation. may
be best illustrated very simply. A man goes into a
rural community, let us say, where there is a general
store. He knows the storekeeper, who has confidence in his integrity, or he has gold or other valuable security, which he deposits with the storekeeper.
It matters not why the storekeeper trusts him. Confidence and trust are at the base of the great struct-
ure of commerce. When that departs men will be
obliged to carry coin about with them, and when
that time comes large transactions, such as are now
of daily, perhaps hourly, occurrence, must cease.
But no one who realizes the deep significance of the
advance of civilization believes that commerce will
cease through the failure of men's confidence and
trust in one another. The man whom I imagine as
going to the simple and rural community desires to
purchase the products of the farmers of the neighborhood. He says to the storekeeper : " These
farmers do not know me, and I have nothing with
which to buy their products. But they know you.
They have confidence in you. They will accept
your promises in payment for their produce. Give
me orders on yourself, and we will share the profits
of the transaction."

Upon this the stranger obtains the orders. For
the community in which he is carrying on his trans-

action these orders constitute a currency. The stranger goes out among the farmers, and finds, as he anticipated, that they are perfectly willing to exchange their products for the orders on the storekeeper. He ships his purchases to the market, and from the proceeds of the sale he pays the storekeeper the amount of the orders issued by him for the purchase of the farmers' products. Besides the amount of the orders, he pays the storekeeper something for the risk he has run and for the accommodation. The amount that he pays is proportioned to the risk if he is the only applicant, and is limited by the amount or profit which the speculator will probably make in the market to which he will send his purchases. In this transaction we have the operations of a bank of discount and of a bank of circulation. The storekeeper takes a receipt from the speculator for the orders which he has given him, and this receipt is in the nature of a promissory note, which may be payable on demand or at the end of a specified time.

The speculator may pay the storekeeper in coin. If he does he must pay the cost of shipping it to him. If he can secure paper currency, however, he uses that. As a rule, he will have money in a bank in the place where he lives, and a check on this bank, especially if the bank certifies that the money to meet it is actually in its possession, will be satisfactory to the storekeeper. As to the orders issued

by the storekeeper, they will come to him in due
time, but he will not have to pay all of them in
money. The farmers trade with him, and some of
them are indebted to him. When he receives one
of his orders from a debtor, he accepts it as a full
or part payment of his account, according to the
amount of each. No money has passed—that is,
no coin has been used in a transaction in which an
order is finally cancelled by a debt due to him who
issued it. The bit of paper calling for, let us say,
$100, was accepted by the farmer in return for his
grain. · He may have used it to buy a horse from
a neighbor, who also had confidence in the storekeeper. That neighbor may have paid a debt to
another. This other may have paid interest with
it on a mortgage held by the storekeeper. Let us
suppose that the storekeeper has issued orders for
$10,000. If $8000 of this goes to the persons in
debt to the storekeeper, or who want goods that he
has, only $2000 will have to be redeemed in actual
money. In the meantime, in the instance of the
$100 order which I have imagined, $100 worth of
grain has purchased a horse, the horse has paid a
debt owed by the seller, and the fourth holder has
paid $100 of interest on his mortgage, and all of
these transactions, aggregating $400, have been car-
ried on with one piece of paper, and without the
use of a single coined dollar.

From what we have seen already, it is clear that

2

persons who insist that hard times come from lack
of money or currency must prove their case, for, if
they are right, there is not only a sufficient supply
of articles in the world, but there is also a desire on
the part of those who own those articles to exchange
with one another, while the only thing that prevents
such an exchange is the lack of an instrument or
vehicle with which to effect it; and this is an im-
probable state of affairs.

IV

In a bank-note the banker makes a promise to pay a definite sum of money to the person who presents it for redemption. The general storekeeper is the banker in the case which I have imagined. He issued orders on himself, which were used as currency. It is quite possible that not one of such orders would ever demand the use of a single coined dollar. It must be recollected that the leading question raised by those who are opposed to a single gold standard is as to the quantity of real money.

Let us assume for the sake of illustration that the storekeeper's $10,000 in orders came finally into the possession of his debtors; that every man who held one of them owed him a sum of money equal to the face value of the order. The result would be that, through the agency of the speculator, the storekeeper would obtain payment of the debts due him. The farmers, by using the orders, would pay their debts in grain, in horses, in old accounts, in interest money, in products of various kinds. Trade would be facilitated by the use of this paper. The speculator himself might not employ any coin in repaying the storekeeper. As we have seen, he might send his check to the storekeeper to pay off the orders he had obtained from him, and it might easily be that the bank on which this check was drawn would hold a note owing by the storekeeper, who had in this way paid for goods which he had purchased. The check would then be used by the storekeeper to pay off the note. Or the check on the bank might be presented to it through another bank, on which, in turn, the first bank might hold a check. Between these two banks there would be a settlement in money of the difference between the two checks. For example: If the check drawn by the speculator to the order of the storekeeper was for $10,500—the $10,-000 of orders and $500 half of the profit of the transaction—it might be sent to a second bank for deposit, or in payment of the storekeeper's note for that amount or for a smaller amount. If the amount of the note were less than the check, the bank would simply give the storekeeper credit for the difference. Not a dollar of money would pass unless the storekeeper desired a settlement, and then he would receive the balance due him in coin, or in another check, or in bills. The check on the first bank would not necessarily be paid in money if it was presented by the second bank; the first bank might, and if the two banks were located in a city it probably would, hold a check against the second bank. I am now speaking of single transactions for the sake of simplicity. The truth is that to fairly represent the transactions between two banks situated in any considerable city, this single illustration would have to be multiplied by tens, or hundreds, or thousands, according to the size of the city and the volume of its business. The demand on the first bank would be for $10,500. If the demand on the second bank held by the first bank was equal to that, there would be simply an offset, and the accounts between the two would be settled without the passing of a single dollar.

In this event we should have this history of the transactions which began with the loan of orders by the storekeepers to the speculator: The speculator having no money, borrowed orders drawn by the storekeeper on himself. These orders were promises to pay. With these orders the speculator purchased products of the neighboring farmers of the aggregate value of $10,000. With the same orders one farmer purchased a horse; another paid a debt; a third paid interest on his mortgage. Other farmers paid rent, repaired their houses, built barns, bought cattle; and finally, all the orders coming into the possession of debtors of the storekeeper, they were employed to cancel their debts, and the orders were destroyed. With $10,000 worth of the storekeeper's orders transactions involving hundreds of thousands of dollars might thus be carried on, and all without the use of a single piece of real money, or even a single bank-note.

On the other side of the transaction we have this state of affairs : The speculator sells the products which he has bought of the farmers. In payment he receives checks, which he deposits in his bank. Let us call it the First National Bank. These checks are orders on other banks. The speculator draws his own check, which is an order on the First National Bank, and sends it to the storekeeper in payment of the original orders. When the check is received the storekeeper is finally paid the debts owing him by the farmers. When the storekeeper receives the check he deposits it in his local bank, and this bank sends it to its corresponding bank in the city in which the First National Bank is located. Then the First National pays to this corresponding bank, the Second, the difference between whatever check is held by it which is an order on the Second, and that which the Second holds against it, which is the speculator's check to the storekeeper. This is the first use of money or bank-notes in all these many transactions.

Not only has nothing but paper been used, but the paper has consisted of promises to pay, in the aggregate, $10,000 in the dealings between the speculator and the farmers, and $10,500 in the dealings between the speculator and the storekeeper through the agency of the banks.

But checks are not the only kind of currency which can be used as a tool for the facilitating of exchange. There are various other forms of credit, into which we need not inquire so fully as we have examined the procession of the checks. The store-keeper may make a record of his claim against the speculator in his books, and by assigning this claim may obtain goods that he needs; or the farmer from whom the speculator buys the grain may take the promissory note of the speculator and by endorse-ment may purchase the horse that he needs; and so, by endorsement after endorsement, the promissory note may act as the vehicle by which many ex-changes are carried on. Or the speculator may draw a bill against a merchant in the city to whom he expects to sell the grain, and use the bill for paying his debt to the storekeeper. There are endless de-vices by which men carry on business without the use of money, and if it should happen that these devices were abandoned, the business of the world would be greatly crippled. Transactions would be-come cumbersome. It would seem almost like go-ing back to the age of barter. As it is, real money is needed only for the settlement of balances, and how little is needed for that may be judged from the foregoing illustrations. The transactions of the Clearing House, New York City, show that $5,000,-000 in cash will clear $100,000,000 of transactions.

V

Thus far we have examined the various kinds of
tools which men employ for the carrying on of business, and we have seen that any tool is a good one
that will be accepted confidently by the various persons whose industry and products are the subjects
of exchange. Let us apply the principle on a larger
scale. This country carries on an enormous business.
Its foreign commerce in merchandise last year
amounted to $1,547,000,000. Seventy-three per cent.
of our exports were agricultural products. How much
money was employed in carrying on this trade?
The exports and imports of gold will not begin to
pay for all this business. In 1894 the total gold
exports amounted to $76,978,061, and the net gold
exports to $4,528,942. In 1893 the net gold ex-
ports from this country amounted to $87,506,463.
Much of the gold that went from this country was
for the payment of debts represented by securities
which the foreign holders sold because they were
afraid that our currency was about to deteriorate, that
we were about to become a silver country. It is evident that our foreign commerce was not entirely car-

ried on with real money, nor did the national banks of the country carry on all their transactions in such money. On October 2, 1894, as we learn from Secretary Carlisle's report, the national banks had loaned $2,007,122,191. But the money of all kinds in the banks amounted to $422,428,192 only. In July, 1895, all the money in the United States amounted to $2,389,000,000. This was a little more than the sum that was then loaned out by the banks. But even this amount was not all used in business. The amount in circulation in July 1894, was $1,662,-000,000. Although the silver men were crying out for money, the country was not using all the money then in existence, and yet, judging from the amount of loans and discounts alone, it was using tools of exchange that represented much more. Moreover, we had and continue to have a greater amount of money per capita than any other country except France, Portugal, the Netherlands, and Belgium. The amount of money in the United States was $24.07 per capita, while Great Britain possessed $19.98 per capita. Our stock of gold is the largest in the world, except that of France. Our stock of silver of full legal tender is actually the largest, if we except India and China. At the same time our stock of uncovered paper is larger than that of any other country except Russia and the South American States. For a long time our society in the money market has been questionable.

The foreign commerce of the country is based on the fact that there are many thousands of foreign people who want our meat, breadstuffs, and cotton, and that there are many thousands of persons in this country who want woollen goods, cotton goods, silks, velvets, iron, and steel ware from Europe, and sugar, tea, coffee, and spices from other parts of the world. These articles are exchanged for one another. The transactions, measured in money, amount to a much greater sum than the money itself which passes between the two countries. The balances only are settled in specie, as already explained. Whatever grand balance there may exist at the end of the year between two countries like Great Britain and the United States does not depend wholly upon the commerce that has been carried on between them, for Great Britain invests a good deal of money in this country in securities, in business concerns, in real estate, so that while what is called the " balance of trade " may be in our favor—that is, we may have exported more goods than we have imported—Great Britain may nevertheless still be our creditor.

Whatever we have imported in goods is wealth. Whatever Great Britain has received from us in gold is a means of gaining wealth. Every piece of cloth, every suit of clothes, every mechanic's tool, every rail, is something that we want and that makes us better off. Every ship-load of grain that England receives from the United States is so much food for the hungry. But if we sold all this grain for gold, and received it, what good would the gold alone do us? It is not a pile of gold that brings prosperity; it is the gratification of our own and others' desires through the exchange of commodities. The world's commerce is the trade of a simple community amplified. It is an exchange of products, and such exchange is facilitated by the use of credit, of mutual confidence, represented largely by bankers' bills of exchange that do not depend for their validity, or for the trust felt in them by the mercantile communities on the two sides of the ocean, either on the amount of gold in the coffers of the bankers, or on the fiat of the government, or on any legal-tender quality bestowed upon them by law, but upon the general belief in the willingness and ability of the persons on whom the bills are drawn to meet them when they are presented for payment.

What is true of simple trade and of foreign commerce is also true of the sale of a man's labor for wages. The man who works with his hands, or the professional man who works with his brains, wants food, raiment, shelter, books, education for his children. He buys all these things with his labor. He digs in the field, writes or paints, argues in the courts, or preaches in the pulpit for these things. He could not go to the tailor, or to the butcher, or the grocer to barter with any assurance of success, whenever he happened to be in want of the several articles in which they deal, for nine times out of ten his services would not be wanted, and he would be as badly off as the man possessed of a store of gold with nothing to buy with it. Therefore he sells his services for money, and the value of his services, the price which he obtains for them, is not in the slightest degree dependent on the amount of money there is in the community, but on the number of people who can render services such as he has to sell, and on the desire of other people for them. If, for example, there were no disputes requiring settlement by the law, a lawyer who should be dependent for his livelihood on a community in which such a state of things existed would starve to death, even if there were millions of idle money stowed away in the local banks.

VI

It has been demonstrated that no nation alone can compel gold and silver to stand on an unnatural and yet equal footing, and we have seen that little coin is actually used in the world's business. Bimetallism has never existed anywhere except in theory, and all the coins and bullion of the one metal on which the currency of any country has rested for the moment have never been needed for the exchanges of commerce. Neither Congress nor any other body can determine how much money is needed. The demands of business alone measure the amount which ought to be in circulation.

Mr. Edward Atkinson estimates that our internal exchanges involve the expenditure of about $35,000,-000,000. The exchanges of the clearing-houses in 1894 involved $45,000,000,000. The sum paid for the transportation of goods over the railroads alone in 1893 was more than $800,000,000. We have $1,662,000,000 of gold, silver, and government and bank paper in circulation. If we add our foreign commerce to Mr. Atkinson's reasonable estimate of the value of our domestic transactions, we have, on the quantitative theory, exchanges demanding the employment of $36,500,000,000 of tools, which is more than twenty times the sum of money and currency in circulation. To sum up this part of the argument, we have never had a coined dollar for every outstanding paper representative of a dollar, and we never shall have. We have never had a dollar in currency for every dollar involved in exchanges, and we do not need any such amount of money any more than a farmer needs ten forty-bushel wagons because he has to deliver 400 bushels of wheat. The quantity of money needed is best settled by the demand for it.

Exchanges between those who produce and those who desire their products have never been, and never will be, checked by lack of legal-tender currency. In the simple community which I have imagined exchanges were facilitated by the use of the storekeepers' orders. Whenever food, fuel, clothes exist, and there is a demand for them, there will be exchange or trade. Men will obtain what they want, and the people who say that trade is stopped because there is not enough coined money to pay for all that is needed are talking nonsense. In 1893 there was a currency famine—that is, the money and currency of the country were not available for trade. Moreover, exchanges were checked, because demand was pretty generally satisfied. Men were able to wait until doubt and uncertainty should cease, and there

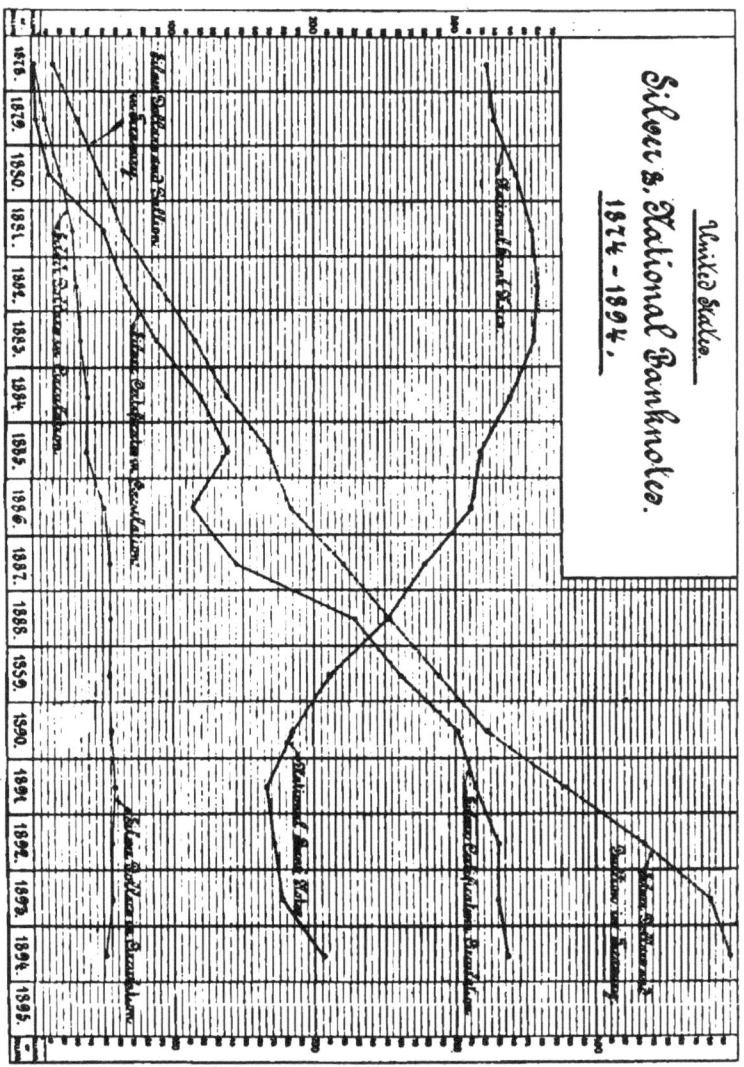

United State

Silver & National Banknotes

1874 - 1894.

should be a return of the general confidence, without which commerce is impossible. But the unwilling-ness of bankers to lend money was met by the in-vention of devices to take the place of the regular and hoarded currency of the country. Cities, banks, and private corporations and firms invented new forms of currency, and exchanges in the necessaries of life went on with the aid of these improvised tools. The country did not need more money, but it did need the removal of a certain fear which kept people from desiring to risk investment of their cash, and there-fore left the cash locked up and out of circulation. That fear was that our money was to be debased, and that our standard of value was to cease to be that which prevails in the rest of the civilized world.

Let us return once more to our simple community. I have assumed that the storekeeper issued orders of the value of $10,000, and that with those orders the people of the community carried on the business of the year. The grower of wheat sold his product to the speculator, and received his price in the orders of the storekeeper. He in turn purchased a horse with the orders he received. The owner of the horse paid a debt. Another paid the interest due on a mort-gage. The money being sufficient for the purposes of the community, if the storekeeper had signed ad-ditional orders he would have had his labor for his pains. The orders would have remained in his drawer. If any more orders were needed he would have been notified at once by the demand for them. If those who received the orders had locked them up, for example, there might have been a demand for new orders — not to supply more currency than there was before, but to take the place of the orders that, by being locked up, had ceased to be currency. But money is never locked up so long as there is a healthy desire for exchanges, and an adequate supply of goods to meet the desire. If, having paid out the whole $10,000 in orders, the speculator should suddenly find some wheat of the existence of which he had not known before, he might go back to the store-keeper and procure more orders, in order that he might purchase it. This is the natural way in which the amount of currency in circulation is increased. Or perhaps some other speculator would borrow orders for the purpose of buying other products of the farmers. The amount of the orders would depend upon the exchanges or trades that could be made through their employment. When all the products of the neighborhood had been purchased, the demand for orders would cease. Of course the amount of storekeepers' orders would vary from year to year. In one year the farmer would raise a great many more bushels of wheat than in the others. Then a dollar might buy more wheat, and the price of the whole crop might not change. Again, the demand for wheat might increase, and more dollars would be required. Two speculators might compete for the crop, and the price might thus advance ; or a second farmer might appear as a rival and the price might go down, or the storekeeper himself might take the farmer's wheat "on account," letting him have goods in the same way, and very few orders would be needed at all. In any case, the storekeeper's orders would equal the requirements of the market; he would never be called upon to redeem them all in coin, no matter what might be the amount of the issue.

It follows, too, that no increase of his money or his orders would affect the course of the exchanges of the community unless the increase were demanded. The speculator would want his wheat, the farmer would want that which would procure him his horse, the owner of the horse would want that which would pay his debt, and so on. A pile of money in the storekeeper's till would not increase the quantity of exchangeable commodities nor the intensity of the desire for them. So long as there were as many orders out as those who used them demanded, so long there would be enough currency in circulation. If the storekeeper had more on hand it would not be used. A farmer would be as wise to send two wagons for one load of hay as the storekeeper would be if he signed orders for two dollars where only one dollar was needed for the transactions of the community. And yet there are men who contend that if you fill the treasury with gold and silver you will hasten transactions and increase prices. That is, if

3

you have no desire to carry your goods to market, you will gain such a desire by providing yourself with some more carts, or if no one needs your goods, the additional carts will create the need. This is also like saying that if no one needs any carpenter-work done, the village carpenter can make work for himself by buying another chest of tools. The difficulty with those who want more money is that they forget what we have learned, that money is a tool to "even-up" trades, and nothing more. Moreover, they think that Congressmen know better than those who are actually engaged in the work of carrying on the business of exchanging goods what amount of money they ought to have. Neither Congressmen nor bankers can tell how much currency is needed by a community. And whoever does try to anticipate the want for currency is in danger of issuing too much, stimulating speculation, and bringing on a panic.

VII

THE undue increase in the amount of money in a country produces panics and brings ruin to business men. If the gold money were increased, the result would be a waste of wealth. If the stock of gold and silver were increased, in addition to this waste of wealth the stock of coin that could be used for money would grow less both in value and in actual amount. The reason of this is that gold would disappear, because men would use that money which is cheapest. The wage-earner would be paid with a silver dollar, because his employer could procure a silver dollar with less exertion or fewer goods than he would have to expend to procure a gold dollar or a paper representative dollar that was payable in gold. The foreigner would send his silver to this country, and our gold would go where it could find employment. If, for example, Mr. Bland had had his way and secured free coinage of silver, our metallic money would have shrunk nearly one-half. In 1895 we had in the United States, according to the estimate of the Treasury, gold of the value of $579,-420,000, and silver of full legal-tender value to the

amount of $548,000,000. If we had become a
silver country, our legal-tender coin would have
shrunk, by reason of the disappearance of gold, from
$1,027,420,000 to $548,000,000. Not only would
the amount of our coin have been reduced by driv-
ing gold out of circulation, but the purchasing power
of the uncovered paper, of which, according to Mr.
Preston, the country had $475,700,000 in 1894, would
also have been reduced. If a paper dollar is made
redeemable in a silver dollar which will buy only one
bushel of wheat, when a gold dollar will buy two
bushels, the paper dollar shrinks to the value of the
silver dollar as a matter of course.

Let us suppose that our storekeeper is himself the
purchaser of the products of his neighbors, and that
he pays for his purchases in coin. Heretofore he
has bought about $100,000 of products every year,
and he has used about $20,000 in coin, the rest of
his payments being made with the goods in his store
which the farmers needed. These goods he has
bought with checks and notes, after the manner
which we have described. But now he secures a
stock of coin equal to the sum involved in his transactions — $100,000. In order to do this he must
buy the coin. Coin cannot be had for nothing. It
is bought with wealth. The storekeeper buys it
with the goods with which he has supplied himself
for the needs of his neighbors. The community is
so much the poorer. It needs just enough money

to pay off the balances that are left after all its
trades of the year are consummated; but the storekeeper's conduct has made it impossible for those
local trades to be carried on. The goods which
constitute his contribution to the trades have been
sent off to secure his coin, and so the farmers
are left without them—having money, it is true, but
money cannot be eaten or worn or used for agricultural implements. It can buy all these things,
but too much of it causes much inconvenience and
expense. In order to procure his stock of money
the storekeeper parted with his goods, and it was
these goods that the farmers really wanted to buy
through the sale of their products. The money was
only used when a farmer either was not ready to buy
the goods or when he wanted something which the
merchant did not have, or when he wanted to put it
away for saving or for other purposes. As it is, the
farmers will be obliged to travel to a distant town to
buy their goods, and the expense and trouble of this
are what the storekeeper's adoption of the quantitative theory of money has cost them. Multiply this
expense by millions, and we will have an idea of the
wasteful extravagance of securing too much money
or dead capital for the whole country.

In 1872, before the passage of the act of 1873
which omitted the silver dollar from the coinage,
there was only $25,000,000 of coin in circulation,
but there was $346,000,000 in greenbacks, $329,-

000,000 in national-bank notes, and $31,500,000 in certificates. Altogether there was $738,000,000 of money in circulation, or about $18.19 for each person in the country. Then followed the panic of 1873, and the amount of money kept on increasing, except in 1876, 1877, and 1878, when it diminished. Silver, it is asserted, was "demonetized," but there was no silver in circulation, except minor coins, in 1872 and 1873. After 1878 the amount of money kept on increasing in the country. Prices went up and down without reference to this increase. Prosperity came back when there was in circulation about $16, and again when there was about $23, for each person in the country, and hard times were upon us when the amount in circulation had grown to be nearly $25 per capita.

In 1894 there was more gold in circulation than ever before in the history of the country. In the panic years, and those immediately preceding them, there were more silver standard dollars in circulation than ever before. The circulation of greenbacks fell off, and that of national-bank notes slightly increased.

All this teaches that the amount of money has very little to do with panics or hard times. The amount of metallic money that should be kept as a reserve for the redemption of paper, or, in other words, the settlement of balances, is best judged by the experiences of the bankers. What the country

Money of the United States.

Year, 1883.

Gold.
$.542,732,063.

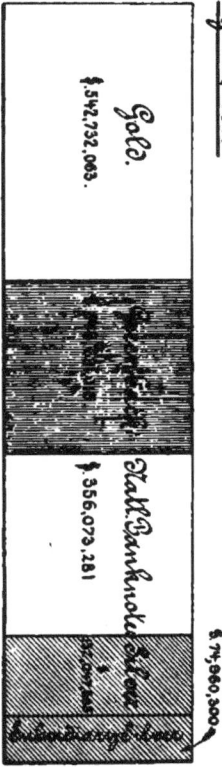

Total. 1,472,494,346. Dollars. | SILVER, 777,007,985 DOLLARS |

State Bank notes
$356,073,281

$74,960,300.

Year, 1895.

Gold.
$636,168,909.

State.
Bank notes
$111,681,035.

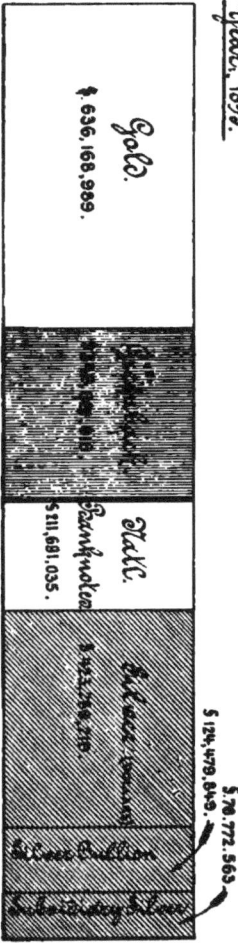

Total. 1,819,082,671 | SILVER, 624,541,631 DOLLARS |

$79,771,563

5,124,479,843.

Silver Bullion

Subsidiary Silver

Per cent.

Silver
1883.
15.4.

Silver
1895.
34.3

needs chiefly is a currency system that can respond
to the demands of business, as the system which I
described in the last article responded to the discovery of the new store of wheat, and to the increase
of the desire to purchase it. This currency ought
to be issued by banks, and there ought to be a certain amount of gold maintained for a reserve. What
that amount ought to be can be best determined by
the peculiar circumstances attending the business of
each bank. In any case it will be comparatively
little. There is much more gold in the country to-
day than is necessary for the settlement of balances
in domestic and foreign commerce. The United
States Treasury tries to maintain $100,000,000 of
gold as a reserve for the redemption of its $346,681,-
000 of greenbacks. It is abundant, and little demand
was ever made upon it until the national credit and
finances were doubted. On this basis the amount of
gold in the country would sustain a paper currency
of about $2,000,000,000, nearly $400,000,000 more
than we now have as the total of all our gold, silver,
and paper in circulation. The procuring of more gold
would be extravagance, for which the producers of
the country would be obliged to pay as the farmers
paid for the storekeeper's folly in the case that I
have imagined. To add silver would be still greater
folly. What is needed is the divorce of government
from the whole system of circulation. If the government does nothing with money except to stamp

its certificate of their value upon coins, then we shall
not have panics bred by the fancies of Congressmen
who think that the real money of the country ought
to be increased, when it is clear from what we have
seen that so long as the standard of value is certain,
the country can be left to regulate the quantity of
its currency by the law of demand and supply.

Panics do not result from too little money, but
generally because an era of speculation has resulted
in many failures. If panics could be relieved by
creating more money, why are they not relieved by
using what exists? In 1893 the loans of the national banks amounted to $1,843,000,000. In 1892 they
had been $2,171,000,000. Panics come not because
men have no tools for the carrying on of trade, but
because there is nothing to trade with, or because
they find out that they have been trading too much,
and then follows a reaction or a lack of confidence
in one another which kills credit, the life of trade.
Our latest panic was not only largely due to the fear
that Congress would do something with our monetary system that would disturb trade and commerce
and injure our credit as a people, but to some causes
that were world-wide in their operation, and to some
that were due to Congressional interference with the
laws of nature that govern exchanges, to protective
tariff laws that hinder and eventually destroy commerce. This country has had a great economic debauch, the terrible penalty for which has been pro-

longed and debilitating. There is money enough in the country. There is gold enough for all the purposes for which we need money.

What the country needs is peace from the political financiers, and from prophets who believe that the more mowing-machines a farmer owns the more hay will he raise.

VIII

It is asserted by the advocates of the free coinage of silver that what is known as the "demonetization" of silver has caused the general decline in prices that has gone on for many years throughout the world. There has, in fact, been no demonetization of silver. In all large commercial countries, except Great Britain, there is to-day a large supply of silver of full legal-tender value. So far as silver has been affected by the laws, additions to this supply have been stopped. Even in Great Britain there is $112,000,-000 of subsidiary silver; in other words, there is in the United Kingdom very nearly as much silver as paper currency. In this country, as we have seen from an examination of the report of the Director of the Mint, there is full legal-tender silver currency amounting to $548,000,000. In France there is $434,300,000 in full legal-tender silver; and in Germany there is $105,000,000. The estimated stock of full legal-tender silver in the whole world is $3,435,-800,000. Therefore prices have not gone down because silver is not used as money of full purchasing power. It is so used. Moreover, in this country the era of low prices has come since silver began to cir-

.culate as legal tender. In 1872 there were no silver dollars in circulation. In speaking of silver I never refer to the subsidiary coin, for it is mere token money used for purposes of change. Silver dollars and certificates began to circulate in 1878. In that year dollars to the amount of $1,209,251 circulated, about $15,000,000 being in the Treasury. Silver certificates of the value of $1,462,600 were engraved and printed, but only $7,080 got into circulation. In 1880 the silver dollars in circulation amounted to $20,110,- 557, and the silver certificates to $5,789,569. In 1890 the amounts of silver coin and certificates in circulation were respectively $56,278,749 and $297,- 556,238—a total of $353,834,987. This amount was slightly increased in the following years, and in 1895 the total amount of silver in circulation in this country was $374,365,741. If low prices are dependent on the scarcity of silver, it would follow that prices ought to have risen during these years. The fact that the prices of nearly all commodities, including silver, fell, however, tends to show that there is no relation between the employment of silver as money and what are known as the market values of commodities.

So far as silver bullion itself is concerned, the laws of the United States intended to increase its price have not had that effect. The average price of silver bullion in 1873 was $1.298 a fine ounce, and a silver dollar, measured by the gold standard, was worth $1.004. The fall in price was not rapid immediately after the enactment of the law of 1873, which was merely the recognition of an existing fact—the non-use of silver as money. The decline was steady, however, and in 1878 Congress undertook to check it by the passage of a law, usually called the Bland law, which made it the duty of the government to purchase and coin every month a certain number of silver dollars. The average price of silver bullion in 1879 was lower than the average price for 1878 had been by about 3 cents an ounce. There was a slight rise in 1880, but after that the decline in prices was resumed, until in 1890 it was about $1.05 an ounce, which was nearly 12 cents higher than the price of 1889. In 1890 the Sherman act was passed. This law was much more "friendly to silver" than the law of 1878 had been, and a good deal was expected from it by the silver men. It added immensely to the government's stock of silver. The amount of silver coin and bullion in the Treasury increased from 1890 to 1895 from $346,597,273 to $495,785,906. The expense to the government also was enormous. Under the act of 1878 the government purchased 291,272,019 ounces, at a cost of $308,279,261. Under the act of 1890 it bought 168,-674,683 ounces, at a cost of $155,931,002. At present prices this mass of bullion is worth about $308,000,-021—a loss of about $156,000,000. These great sums were paid by the tax-payers of this country for the purpose of maintaining silver as a money metal;

Production & Price of Silver.

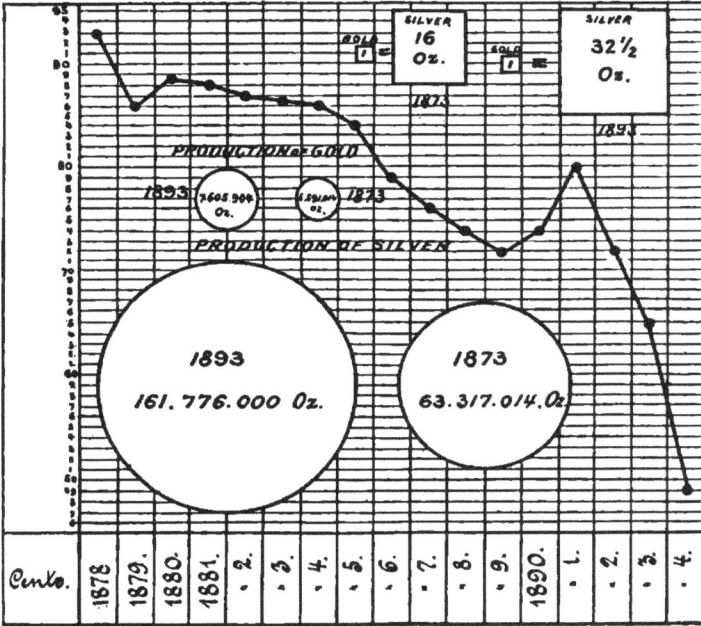

SILVER
16
Oz.

SILVER
32½
Oz.

GOLD 1 =

GOLD 1 =

1873

1893

PRODUCTION of GOLD

1893 7,605,904 Oz. 6,591,247 Oz. 1873

PRODUCTION OF SILVER

1893
161,776,000 Oz.

1873
63,317,014 Oz.

Cents. | 1878 | 1879. | 1880. | 1881. | - 2. | - 3. | - 4. | - 5. | - 6. | - 7. | - 8. | - 9. | 1890. | - 1. | - 2. | - 3. | - 4.

and what was the result? In the first place, the efforts to thus establish silver created a doubt as to our
credit, and helped to bring on a panic, and the President was compelled to call Congress together in an
extra session for the purpose of repealing the law that
was the source of so much trouble. In the second
place, they did not restore prices. Silver itself continued to fall. In 1891 it sold for about 99 cents
an ounce; 1892, for 87 cents; in 1893, for 78 cents;
in 1894 the price fell below 60 cents; and now its
price is about 67 cents.

The effect of these experiments with silver shows
conclusively that the amount of money in the country
has no influence on prices. We have seen how the
total amount of all kinds of currency has increased,
and also the increase in the amount of silver alone,
both in circulation and in the Treasury, since 1873.
Notwithstanding this increase in the amount of money, prices have gone down. Middling cotton brought
20 cents in 1873; it brought $6\frac{94}{100}$ cents in 1894; it
fell to $5\frac{9}{16}$ cents in February, 1895, and is now back to
$6\frac{3}{8}$ cents. Sheetings have been reduced from 13 cents
to 5 cents a yard, standard prints, from 11 to 5 cents;
wool, from prices ranging from 47 to 70 cents to
prices ranging from 19 to 23 cents, according to
quality and season. Prices were not increased by increase of money, nor by the passage of laws friendly
to silver. The act of 1878 did not check the decline,
while the act of 1890, if it produced any effect, must

have expedited it, for prices fell all the faster after the passage of that law. Wheat and corn rose a little after 1878 until 1882, but their prices fell in 1883, without any connection with silver legislation, or even with the price of silver, for silver continued to decline while wheat and corn were rising, as the following table will show:

	Silver per ounce.	Wheat per bushel.	Corn per bushel.
1879	$1.123	$1.212	49.8 cents.
1880	1.145	1.270	55.1 "
1881	1.138	1.318	63.1 "
1882	1.136	1.278	80.1 "

It will be seen from this table that even the prices of corn and wheat are not interdependent.

In extending our inquiry into the relation between the amount of money in existence and the prices of commodities, recent statistics published by recognized authorities are of great value. The silver agitators are complaining of low prices, and holding that dear food, clothing, and house rent indicate prosperity. How different is this proposition from that usually advanced? It is wholly opposed to the position held by the protectionists, who insisted that their tariff had not increased prices, but had reduced the cost of the necessaries of life by increasing competition. In the tariff discussion both sides were in favor of cheap food, clothes, tools, and houses. But when the same men talk in favor of the free coinage of silver,

they are against cheapness and in favor of high
prices. It would seem as though the whole discussion were a hollow mockery.

. Mr. Edward Atkinson has recently presented in the
Forum the truth about prices as they are shown by
the statistics gathered by Augustus Sauerbeck, by
Labor- Commissioner Wright, computed and compared by Professor Falkner, of Johns Hopkins Uni-
versity, on the assumption that prices were at par in
1860. In that year a silver dollar was worth more
than a gold dollar under our laws. Compared with
the price in 1860 (100), silver was 95.3 in 1845, 97.3
in 1850, and 100 in 1855. In the same years meat
had risen from 79.4 in 1845 to 104.7 in 1855. Other
food had risen from 82.8 to 114.5. Clothes had
grown cheaper. While the gold price of silver was
increasing 4.7 points, the price of meat increased 25.3
points ; other food, 31.7 points ; that of clothes fell
2.4 points ; and the average of all prices had increased 10.3 points. In the mean time wages increased 11.2 points. So while the price of silver was
going up, the prices of other commodities went up
faster, and the purchasing power of wages became
greater.

The price of silver began to fall about 1866, and
it has kept on falling ever since. In 1870, three
years before the demonetization " crime," it had
fallen 1.8 below the 100 standard of 1860. But
every other commodity had advanced. Meat was

174.3 when silver was 98.2; other food was 146.3; clothes were 139.4; while wages were 162.2. Therefore at this time, at all events, the prices of food, of clothes, and of labor did not fall with the price of silver. There was no silver in circulation, and the changes in its price had not affected the general market. Then as now, also, the purchasing power of wages was increasing. Not a necessary of life was so cheap in this country in 1870 as it had been in 1860, but the labor that could have purchased $66 worth of goods in 1865 purchased more than $114 worth in 1870.

Silver continued to fall. In 1875 it was 92.2, compared with the scale of 100 in 1860. At the same time all other prices had gone down, and they have continued to go down, until within the last few months, when they are rising again. But it is to be noticed that while the cost of commodities decreased, the purchasing power of wages increased, until it had risen from 114.1 in 1870 to 172.1 in 1890.

The fall in prices has not been confined to this country. It has taken place in Great Britain as well. It is due to better and cheaper methods of production and transportation. The tendency of prices has been the same in gold and in silver countries. The amount of money has had no influence upon it, but modern progress is accountable for most of the decline, and so-called overproduction for some of it. How much the inventions of cheaper and better

methods of production have accomplished in bringing about a reduction of prices is shown by the decline in the cost of metals and implements to the
producer, to effecting which the inventive genius of
the world, and especially of this country, has chiefly
directed itself. Representing the gold price of metals and implements in 1860 by 100, in 1870 it was
127.8 in paper, and in 1890 it was 74.9 in gold. In
England, at the same time, the price fell from 100 to
87.4. The causes that bring about reductions in
price are shown by these statistics of production : In
1860, less than 7,000,000 tons of iron were produced
in the world. In 1892 the production of iron had
increased to 26,000,000 tons, the United States alone
producing 9,157,000 tons. What wonder that iron
is cheaper than it was? Silver has grown cheaper
for the same general reason that has governed the
price of iron. In 1873 the world produced 63,267,-
000 ounces of silver. It was worth $82,120,000. If
it had been coined it would have made only $81,800,-
000. In 1893, the world's product of silver was
161,776,100, and it was worth $126,185,300. But
if it had been coined it would have made $209,165.-
000. Can any one imagine a greater swindle than
such a creation of false values would have been?
Iron that was worth $100 in 1860 could be bought
for $75 in 1890. Suppose that the law had com-
pelled every farmer to pay for the iron in his agricultural implements at the price prevailing in 1860 ?
4

Would there not have been a revolution? Why should the laws treat the silver-miners any better than they treat the iron-miners?

In 1874 this country produced 850,148,500 bushels of corn; in 1893 it produced 1,619,496,131 bushels. In 1874 we produced 308,102,700 bushels of wheat; in 1893 we produced 396,131,725 bushels. In 1875 we produced 3,827,845 bales of cotton; in 1894 we produced 7,549,817 bales. These are potent reasons why corn, wheat, and cotton are cheaper. Another reason is that transportation charges are cheaper. In 1875 the freight charge on a bushel of wheat sent by lake and canal from Chicago to New York was about 11¼ cents; in 1894 it was less than 4½ cents. If sent by rail the charge in 1875 was 24 cents; in 1894 it was about 13 cents.

Perhaps the most striking contribution to this discussion of the relations between the employment of silver as money and prices has been made by Mr. Upton, formerly Assistant Secretary of the Treasury. He makes his compilation from the report of a committee consisting of Senators Aldrich, Allison, Hiscock, Jones (Nevada), Harris, and Carlisle. The committee computed the average prices of nine principal agricultural articles—barley, corn, cotton, hemp, oats, meats, rye, tobacco, and wheat. It was found that in 1860, when the average price of these nine articles was 100, the price of the bullion in a silver dollar was 104.6. In 1870 the price of the nine agricultural products had risen to 107.7, but the price of the silver dollar had fallen to 102.3. In 1875 silver fell still further, to 92.2, but the price of the agricultural products increased to 116.8. In 1891 the price of silver had fallen 30.5 points, and the average price of the other commodities 1.6 points.

So we see that while silver has been going down, the prices of all other products have also gone down, but not so steadily nor so much as that of silver, and that at times when silver fell the prices of other articles rose. We have also seen that prices of agricultural products rose after the so-called demonetization of silver, although the price of silver fell. The price of silver continued to fall after the acts of 1878 and 1890, which were passed to advance it. On the other hand, the average price of the nine articles already mentioned fell from 116.8 to 102.9 after the act of 1878, and rose from 87.9 to 98.4 after the act of 1890.

Still further evidence that prices are not affected by the amount of money in the country is furnished by the commercial and financial history of the present year.

There is much evidence in the recent history of the country that while the amount of money in circulation, or in existence, has little to do with prices, and that trade and commerce are only temporarily checked by lack of currency, the character of our currency has a strong influence upon our prosperity.

We know, for example, that the mad speculation inspired by the cheapness of our paper currency led directly to the disastrous and distressing panic of 1873, and that to the apprehension felt by the holders of our securities was largely due the panic of 1893. In 1878 the country was on a gold basis. Prices had begun to fall about 1865; and that decline was not due, of course, to any war on silver, or to any currency legislation whatever. In 1877 there was slightly less money in the country than there had been before, in consequence of the redemption of greenbacks. In 1878, however, the amount of money began to increase. In 1879 there was in existence in money and legalized substitutes for money $5 more for each person in the country than there had been in 1878; but only $1.43 of this increase got into circulation. The government (in other words, the tax-payers) had paid the expense of creating $5 in currency for every $1.43 demanded by the business interests. In 1894 the amount of money in the country was about $19 per capita more than it was in 1877—that is, it had a good deal more than doubled. But the business of the country at the end of those sixteen years, as shown by its demand for currency, needed only $9 per capita more than was required by it in 1877. In that period there had been created money and currency to the amount of $1,657,000,000, in addition to that which existed at

Prices of Wheat, Corn and Cotton.

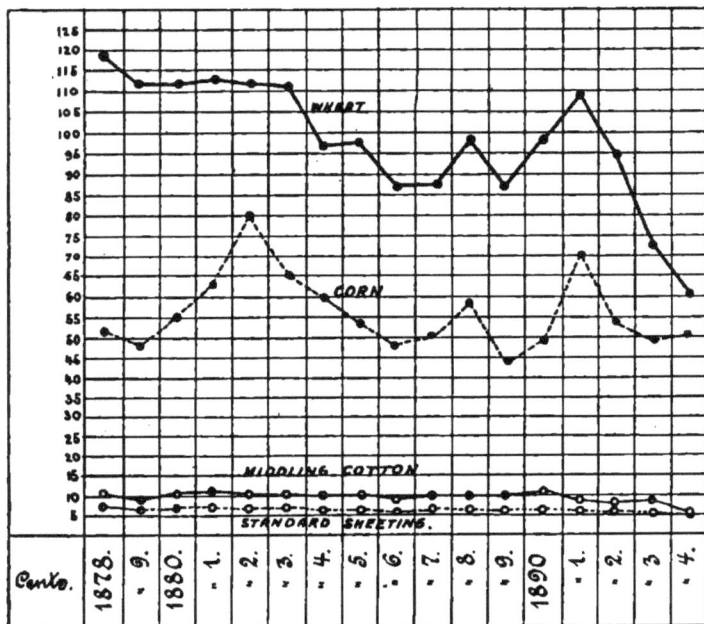

the beginning of the period, to meet an increased demand for $937,494,000. And this enormous increase of money and currency, wasteful and extravagant as it was, costing the tax-payers enormous sums of money, did not check the fall of prices, which was due to the lower cost of production and distribution, the result of the wonderful inventive genius, enterprise, and energy of the age.

What was the effect, however, of the resumption of specie payments—the mere declaration that the country was on a gold basis, and would redeem its promissory notes in coin of the legal standard? Let us examine the prices prevailing in two periods. One period is from 1878 to 1890, when the Sherman law was passed for the purpose of compelling the government to buy substantially the whole product of American silver-mines, and to add its fictitious value to the currency of the country. The other is the period immediately after the passage of that law.

FIRST PERIOD.			SECOND PERIOD.		
Articles.	1878. Prices. Cents.	1890. Prices. Cents.	Articles.	1890. Prices. Cents.	1894. Prices. Cents.
Middling cotton.....	11.22	11.07	Middling cotton....	11.07	6.94
Standard sheetings..	7.8	7.0	Standard sheetings.	7.0	5.11
Shirtings...........	11.	10.9	Shirtings..........	10.9	9.5
Print cloths	3.44	3.34	Print Cloths	3.34	2.75
Wheat	118.8	98.3	Wheat.............	98.3	61.1
Corn	51.4	48.1	Corn	48.1	60.9

It is clear from these two tables that prices were steadier when there was no question as to the value of our money, when the irredeemable paper had

been converted into a gold note. Even the attempt
to depreciate the currency through the silver act of
1878 did not disturb the markets. The reason is
that the country was rich enough to pay the cost of
adding millions of silver dollars each year to the
amount in the Treasury without suffering disastrous consequences, and silver did not enter into the
circulation, either in the form of coined dollars or
certificates, before 1888. In that year the amount of
silver certificates out was $200,760,000, while silver
dollars amounting to $55,527,000 were in circulation.
Since then the amount of silver certificates in circulation has increased to $319,700,000, while the
amount of silver dollars that are out has fallen to
$52,000,000.

It is hardly worth while to furnish other facts and
statistics to prove that prices of commodities do
not depend on the quantity of money in existence.
I have shown that the rise and fall of prices have
not depended on the quantity of money; that the
quantity of money has been actually increased and yet
prices have gone down; that silver has fallen while
prices of other commodities have risen; that laws
have been passed to increase the value of silver and to
advance other prices without accomplishing either ob-
ject; that prices have been steadier when the country
was frankly on a gold basis than when it was encouraging the employment of silver as legal-tender money;
and that the effort to maintain silver has much more

than doubled the quantity of money in the country, has added to the currency nearly twice as much money as the increased business of the country has absorbed, and all this, of course, at an enormous cost to the tax-payers.

Prices are determined by demand and supply. To go back to our simple community, if the wheat-grower has a bad year and raises only half the usual crop of grain, his crop will be worth twice as much per bushel in horses, corn, clothes, as in a full crop year. He will get twice as many dollars per bushel, other things being equal, as he usually receives. Each bushel of wheat will buy twice as much as a bushel brought last year. But the whole crop will not buy any more than the whole of the larger and cheaper crop brought. If there is a falling off in other crops, or if clothes and other merchandise in the storekeeper's stock are dearer in consequence of an increased demand or an increase in the cost of production or transportation, the farmer's bad crops will bring less to him in what he needs—that is, in what he uses his money to procure—although he receives actually more money. If the storekeeper's goods advance in price he will receive more money, but that money will buy less of the produce of the farmer. What has really happened throughout the world has been already indicated, and that has happened especially in this country, which is so amply blessed in material wealth that it prospers in spite

of the follies and ignorance of those who makes its
laws, and who tamper with its economic and monetary systems with a hardy recklessness that is born
of ignorance of the fact that exchange is governed
by the laws of nature, which cannot be successfully
opposed by those of man. The necessaries of life
have been growing cheaper while it has been growing
easier to earn them. Even now, when prices are going
up, when the iron-mills find it difficult to keep up with
the orders that are pouring in upon them, wages have
been advanced in the manufacturing establishments
of the country—in the cotton and woollen mills of
New England and the iron and steel mills of Penn-
sylvania.

IX

It was a free-coinage advocate who invented the theory that cheap necessaries of life are curses. Until this curious doctrine was promulagated, it had been supposed that cheap bread meant prosperity— that the only price that rose with the coming of better times was the price of labor. And now when we have the conditions that make for prosperity we hear that the world has been mistaken, and that the wage-earner will be the happier when his food and tools cost him more; that the farmer will once more smile when he pays war prices for his clothes, his lumber, and his agricultural implements. As to the farmer, he should bear in mind that while the prices of some of his products have decreased, the prices of others have risen since 1873; that pig-iron, which is the chief material of his reaper and other implements, sells for about $13 a ton, although in 1873 it sold for about $43; that steel rails have fallen from $120 to $24 a ton; that the freight charges on his products are less, as I have already shown, by at least 50 per cent.; that while the price of his wheat has been reduced about 50 per cent., the price of his corn has risen;

and that the price of mess pork is about the same
as it was twenty years ago, while he pays about
60 per cent. less for the cottons that he wears and
uses in his house, about 66 per cent. less for his sugar, more than 80 per cent. less for his illuminating
oil, and that his clothes and shoes do not cost more
than a third of what he paid twenty years ago.

There is only one class that would apparently be
benefited by cheap money and dear goods, and that
is what is called the " debtor class," but the debtor
who fancies that he is to be ultimately benefited in
this dishonest way is grievously mistaken.   According to the census report of 1890, the number of
mortgaged farms in the country was one in five.   In
the South the number was between two and three per
cent.   The mortgage indebtedness in the Northwest
was for lands and improvements.   The greater part of
this indebtedness was owing in the Northwest, where
land has risen in value, this increase alone being far beyond the amount of the mortgage indebtedness.   Are
we to change our currency system, and to establish a
fluctuating and dangerous currency which will bring
disaster, the mere threat of which has already produced a panic from which we have not yet recovered,
in order that the owners of these valuable farms may
pay their creditors less purchasing power than they
borrowed?   It would be like this: Thirty years ago
a pioneer borrowed $2500, and with it bought and
improved a hundred acres of land in Wisconsin.

His land and buildings are now within a short dis-
tance of a thriving town, and are worth $20,000. He
still owes the money that he borrowed, preferring to
pay 7 or even 10 per cent. interest for money on
which he can make a profit of from 15 to 25 per cent.
Or it may be that with all his prosperity, and notwithstanding the growing value of his lands, he is
not often in command of ready cash, or he may be
extravagant. Whatever the reason may be, he is
still in debt, and he wants cheap money with which
to pay his creditor. He wants to drive gold out of
circulation, to introduce silver through free coinage,
two dollars of which will purchase only as much of
his products as could be bought by one of the dollars
that he borrowed. At present prices he owes the
man who has enabled him to make $20,000, less the
$2500 of capital that he lent him, the equivalent of
about 4000 bushels of wheat, and he wants the money system changed so that he can pay with about
2000 bushels. It is hardly probable that the four
farmers out of every five who owe nothing will consent to incur the perils of free coinage of silver in
order to permit the one debtor to pay 2000 bushels
of wheat where 4000 are honestly due. Nor is it
probable that many of the debtors themselves will
ask such a dishonest favor when they come fully to
understand the real nature of their request.

But the silver men say that the cheaper money will
benefit those who are paying their debts every year—

not mortgage debtors only. How many of the community do these debtors number? One would suppose that the majority of the people of this country were in debt to the minority and to foreigners, who ought to be thankful if they are swindled by our free and independent debtors. As a matter of fact, out of annual payments and receipts made and acknowledged in the business of this country, amounting to about $50,000,000,000, only about $1,500,000,000, or 3 per cent., is paid and received in settlement of debts, so that we are asked to debase our currency, to make our money cheap, to increase the burdens of the producers, the wage-earners, the merchants, and the professional men, to incur the terrors and disasters of a fluctuating medium of exchange, and to add greatly to the dangers of trades and exchanges involving $50,000,000,000 in order that persons owing $1,500,000,000 may pay in fewer goods or effects than they owe.

So much for the debtor argument, or rather outcry. It is a dishonest argument, and is very properly supported by a dishonest pretence that most of the country is on the verge of bankruptcy, and that the government should save the great majority of the people from the oppression of those who demand just payment of that which is their due. Such an outcry would have produced very little effect on the minds of the American people if it had not been complicated with false pretences as to the causes of low

HIGH-TONED, HIGH-STRUNG U. S. (TO DIOGENES). "ANY INSINUA-
TION? YOU GOLD BUG! YOU SHYLOCK! YOU BLOATED BOND-
HOLDER! YOU CAPITALIST! YOU ARE PURCHASED BY WALL-
STREET SHARKS."

prices and as to the pretended conflict of interests between the different sections of the country. There is no such conflict. The interests of all sections of the country are the same. The man who lends money is deeply and selfishly interested in the prosperity of the man who borrows. He desires him to make money in order that he may pay his interest and debt. One word more concerning mortgage debtors. Much the larger part of this debt is now overdue. The amount of the mortgage debts in this country is about $6,000,000,000, and of this payment of at least $4,000,000,000 could be demanded to-morrow. Suppose that free coinage of silver were adopted, and gold were driven out of circulation. Silver would pass then at its real worth, and as it has been continuously depreciating for a long time, the mortgage creditors would greatly fear its still further depreciation. The result would be that a large part of these mortgages would be foreclosed at once. Has the "debtor class" taken this into account?

X

THE notion that low prices have been compelled
by the alleged "demonetization" of silver in 1873,
and that they have caused general distress, has been
sufficiently answered. Low prices have not resulted
from a disuse of silver as money, for there has been
an increase in the amount of silver money since 1873;
nor from a decrease of the quantity of money in existence and in circulation, for there has been an increase of that. They are due to other causes, which
have been explained, and they have aided instead of
retarded the welfare of the people. A bushel of
grain buys more than it bought twenty years ago,
and a day's work buys much more than it purchased
when the pretended "crime against silver" was com-
mitted.

It remains to examine some further evidences of
the country's prosperity during the last twenty years.
Not only can a day of effort obtain more of the necessaries and luxuries of life, but the public burdens
have been decreased and consumption has increased,
while if there has been a slight increase in taxes, it
is because of the expenditures of local governments,

for which the people themselves are responsible.
Local taxes may represent increased prosperity. The
community may add to their common expenditure
because they feel better able to pay for permanent
improvements or communal luxuries. Taxes may,
and often do, grow by reason of the carelessness or
corruption of local authorities, but if the people of
any community do not desire to be burdened by the
ignorance or corruption of their servants, they have
the remedy in their own hands.

The signs of the increased wealth and prosperity
of the people of the United States since 1873 are
abundant. The people of this country, as a whole,
have not been distressed either by the currency act
of 1873 or by any other cause. Here and there individuals or classes may have suffered by over or
extravagant production, or by the growth of competition in special industries and in foreign countries.
Great distress and disturbance have been wrought
by the acts of 1878 and 1890, which were intended
to "rehabilitate silver." But during the period from
1873 to 1894 the people reduced the interest-bear-
ing public debt from $1,710,483,950 to $635,041,-
890, thereby saving nearly $73,000,000 a year in in-
terest alone. The result of the silver act of 1878
was to immediately increase the debt by about
$83,000,000, and the annual interest charge by
$1,500,000, while the act of 1890, and accompanying
extravagant appropriations, increased the debt from

$585,029,330 in 1892 to $635,041,890 in 1894. At the same time the debt on which no interest is paid decreased, from 1873 to 1879, from $472,069,333 to $410,835,742. After the passage of the Bland-Allison act in 1878, and of the Sherman act of 1890, and up to 1892, it increased from $410,835,742 to $1,000,648,939. Since the repeal of the Sherman act this debt has been reduced. Thus the people have paid off about $1,100,000,000 of their interest-bearing debt since 1873, and the efforts to "rehabilitate silver" have alone checked the work of wiping out this burden.

In 1873 the net deposits in the national banks of the United States were $673,400,000; in 1894 they were $2,019,300,000. I have not the data of savings-banks prior to 1883. In that year their deposits amounted to $1,024,856,787. In 1894 they amounted to $1,777,933,242.

I have already spoken of our increased production of agricultural wealth. In 1873 this country exported cotton goods of the value of $2,947,528. In 1894 its exports of cottons, had increased in value to $14,340,886. In 1873 the country produced 264,314,148 gallons of crude petroleum, and in 1894 its production had increased to 2,033,331,-972 gallons. In 1873 the total product of cane-sugar in this country was 134,832,493 pounds; in 1894 it was 610,825,618 pounds. In 1873 our wool product was 158,000,000 pounds; in 1894 it was

298,057,384 pounds. In 1874 we manufactured 2,401,262 tons of pig-iron; in 1893 we made 7,124,-502 tons.

If we examine the statistics of this period, so prosperous in spite of adverse tariff and silver legislation, with reference to the population of the country, we find that they are quite as encouraging. Increased wealth, easier circumstances, are shown by the lightening of the burdens of debt to the individual, and by his greater consumption of the necessaries and luxuries of life.

In 1873 the public debt was a little more than $50 for each individual in the country; in 1894 it was about $13. The per capita consumption of cotton increased from 15.19 to 15.91 pounds; of sugar, from 39.8 to 66.4 pounds; of coffee, from 6.87 to 8.01 pounds; of malt liquors, from 7.21 to 15.18 gallons. The consumption of wheat and distilled spirits fell off, and the consumption of raw wool remained about stationary. The revenue of the post-office increased from 55 cents to $1.10 per capita, and the expenditures from 70 cents to $1.24. The expenditures for public schools increased from $5.95 to $8.31 per capita, 1893 being the last year for which data are available on this subject.

I have already stated the decline in the cost of transportation within this period. In 1873 the average toll on a telegraph message was 62½ cents, and the profit on it was 19.1 cents. In 1894 the average toll was 30½ cents, and the profit was slightly less than 10 cents.

In 1870 the true value of real and personal property in New England and the Middle States was $15,290,032,687, or $1,243 per capita; in 1890 it was $21,435,491,864, or $1,232 per capita. In the Southern Atlantic States, the value in 1870 was $2,249,280,146, or $384 per capita; in 1890 it was $5,132,980,666, or $579 per capita. It will be seen that the South has been especially blessed with increase of wealth since the commission of the "crime of 1873." The same is true of the Middle West, including the Dakotas, Nebraska, and Kansas. In the twenty years the property of that section increased in value from $9,542,053,355 to $25,255,-915,549, or from $735 to $1,129 per capita. The story of growing prosperity in these twenty years is repeated in the Middle South, including Kentucky and Tennessee, the Gulf States, Arkansas, Oklahoma, and the Indian Territory. The value of property increased there from $2,152,182,361 to $6,401,281,-019, or from $334 to $569.* In the Northwestern and Pacific States the census statistics tell a far more wonderful story of growth in wealth and prosperity. In 1870 the total property of those States and Territories was valued at $834,969,958, or $843 per capita; in 1890 it had increased to $6,811,422,-099, or $2,250 per capita. The total value of the

* Omitting the true valuation of the Indian Territory.

real and personal property in the United States in these twenty years increased from $30,068,518,507 to $65,037,091,197, or from $780 to $1,036 per capita.*

In the mean time taxes have increased and decreased in the various sections of the country, as will appear from the following table, which shows the per capita rates of taxation:

Divisions.	1870.	1890
New England and Middle	$10.07	$10.29
South Atlantic.	3.97	3.69
Middle West.	7.42	8.13
Middle South	4.18	3.35
Northwest and Pacific	10.51	13.67
United States	7.28	7.53

Taxes have been reduced per capita in the South, and slightly advanced in the whole country.

In the last decade the total State, county, and local indebtedness has increased in the whole country from $1,123,278,647 to $1,135,210,442, but it has decreased per capita from $22.40 to $18.13.

The free-silver man's tale of woe seems to be unsupported by the facts of the country's industrial history.

* Omitting the true valuation of the Indian Territory.

XI

In all that I have said thus far, I have simply alluded to the subject of international bimetallism. I have refrained from dwelling on it because it is remote from the discussion of the day. Whether by the concurrence of all the nations of the world 16 or 15½ ounces of silver could be made equal to one ounce of gold, it seems clear to me that the world does not need the amount of metal money that the universal free coinage of silver might provide, for it may be at once assumed that as the mints of the world would thereby become the best customers of the silver mines, most of the silver mined would be made into coin. Perhaps the whole world would go to a silver basis. No one can foresee exactly what would happen, but if the expectation of the bimetallists were realized there would be a great increase in the amount of metal money in the world, and if I am right in believing that I have succeeded in showing that such an increase is not needed, the metal money added to the present store would represent just so much wasted effort, energy, and wealth. The world can no more procure metal money for nothing than

can a single country. If the storekeeper provides
himself with gold and silver to carry on the transactions of his neighborhood when his own notes will
accomplish the task, he and the community will lose
the amount of useful wealth or merchandise with
which he purchases his useless hoard of silver and
gold. As it is with the storekeeper so it has been
with this country, and so it will be with the world.
I have already shown how many millions the United
States have lost through the compulsory purchase of
silver, and how much greater has been the increase
in our stock of metal money than in the demands of
our business for it. If our village storekeeper should
follow the example of the United States and should
expend all his wealth for gold and silver coin, trade
between the farmers and himself, either direct or carried on through the medium of the speculator, would
come to an end, or at least be greatly decreased.
And this would be a costly experiment for the merchant whose wealth, instead of being in goods which
he could sell at a profit, would be in idle coin, which
the farmers did not at all want. Of course trade
would then go on between the farmers and the wiser
merchants of a neighboring community, and the
farmers would be obliged to pay for the transportation
of their products to the distant point, and for the
transportation back of the goods that they needed,
and for which they would exchange their own products. As I have already said, the farmer pays the

cost of transportation both ways. There is another thing that might happen. Our original shopkeeper might be a cunning man wishing to make money out of the troubles of his rural neighbors. He might sell his goods for coin in order to lend the farmers money to transport their products, or by way of advance on their crops, in order that they might purchase what they needed before they had earned the money by selling their products. Here is another way by which the farmer would be obliged to pay for the folly or the cunning of the storekeeper in buying unnecessary coin with his goods, the goods that were needed in the homes of the farmers.

It may be assumed that the man who wants money to enable him to exchange his products or his day's work for the necessaries or luxuries of life, is the man who pays the cost of extravagant money schemes; and bimetallism, if it shall be adopted, will prove no exception to the rule. Bimetallism has never existed in practice in the world's history. It has been decreed by law, but whenever two metals have been made legal tender the cheaper has invariably driven the dearer metal out of circulation. In our own country gold was undervalued from 1792 to 1834, and we had nothing but silver, and cheap foreign silver at that, as circulating coin, and after that silver disappeared, because, at the established ratio, silver was too valuable to be coined into dollars. At the present time, if the government should say that 16

ounces of silver shall be accepted by the wage-earner,
the professional man, the merchant, and the manu-
facturer, in return for services and goods that are
worth 1 ounce in gold, it would cheat the producers
and working-people of the country out of about 16
ounces of silver on every such transaction, for an
ounce of gold is now worth about 32 ounces of silver.
Perhaps all the nations of the world together might
make 16 ounces of silver equivalent to 32 ounces, but
if the attempt should be made, any one of the nations might break the agreement, and then all would
be confusion in the world's monetary system. And
again, if all the governments of the world, agreeing,
can make 16 ounces equal to 32 ounces, why waste
15 ounces? why not make 1 ounce equal to 32?
Why use silver or gold? Why not adopt the iron
unit of the ancient Spartans?

I am not trying to discuss the question of international bimetallism, but simply to indicate the uncer-
tainties into which the adoption of such a scheme
would plunge us. International bimetallism is as
much an intellectual vice as is the game of chess
when it is played too much. Ingenious minds like to
speculate concerning it, and they enjoy the excite-
ment of chasing their own fancies. But international
bimetallism is not a practical or immediate issue.
What this country and the world want above all
things, and just now especially, when business seems
to be reviving, is to leave existing monetary condi-

tions as they are, so far as the metals are concerned. Above all else, everything that is uncertain is dangerous.

So far as the United States are concerned, it is certain, for it has been demonstrated, that we cannot maintain bimetallism alone; that we have gone beyond the danger point in expending revenue and wealth in the attempt to maintain what we call the parity of the two metals. The immediate issue before the country is not international bimetallism, but silver monometallism. If any considerable body of people want international bimetallism, there will be ample time and opportunities to discuss that question when there is a conference of the nations. As it is, our people are not concerned with it at all. All that we have to decide now is this: Shall Congress pass a law which will compel the tax-payers of this country to buy of the silver-mine owners 16 ounces of silver with goods and services that ought to command 32 ounces? Shall our whole currency system be confused by a double standard which means silver monometallism? Shall prices be measured in a fluctuating medium? Shall our foreign exchanges be complicated to the profit of the money-broker and the loss of the producer and the working-man? Shall we have a money that may scale down debts, but which will destroy our credit, drive capital out of the country, especially from those parts of the country which need development, and transfer the United States

THE COMRADES THAT FREE COINAGE WOULD MAKE FOR UNCLE SAM

from among the great commercial nations and make it the monetary comrade of China, Japan, India, and the South and Central Americas? These are the questions which the people of this country must answer at once, and any one who, under these conditions, undertakes to talk to them about international bimetallism is their enemy, for he is trying to deceive and confuse them.

XII

In conclusion, I will restate some of the propositions that I have laid down and endeavored to sustain in these papers. I began with the proposition that money is not a good in itself, but only as it easily and conveniently procures for its possessors what they need or desire. It saves the trouble and expense of barter. It represents food, raiment, shelter, and other necessaries of life as well as its luxuries.

The quality that money should possess ought to be clear to every one. It must be honest money. If it is metal it must be intrinsically worth the sum it professes. If it is paper it must be redeemable in the amount called for by its face. It must mean what it says. It must not only actually possess these qualities, but those who are asked to accept it in return for their products and goods must believe that it does. In the simple community the storekeeper's orders possessed these qualities, and they passed as money. So bank paper passes in the country in which the bank is situated, whose people believe that the bank is sound. But in international commerce, gold is the only money that is universally recognized, and it is necessary, therefore, for this country and for all countries that carry on commerce to accept gold as the standard of value. Otherwise there must be confusion arising from fluctuations in exchange, which would be largely due to fluctuations in the price of any other metal than gold that became the standard of value of the country departing from the gold standard.

Whatever may be said in favor of international bimetallism, international bimetallisn is not an imminent question. The first question that this country must answer is whether it, will abandon the monetary system which prevails among the stronger nations of the world, and adopt that which prevails among the weaker nations, whether it will abandon gold and take silver as its standard. It has been proved that it cannot alone maintain silver. The panic of 1893 demonstrated this to intelligent minds. It has also been proved that it cannot alone maintain the price of silver, which has been falling for nearly thirty years. The failure of the attempts to do so through the acts of 1878 and 1890, is a signal proof of the inability of this country, acting alone, to make sixteen ounces of silver equal to one ounce of gold, when in the markets of the world thirty-two ounces of silver are equal in value to one ounce of gold. The only ground on which the single silver standard could be maintained is that we may be independent of Europe; but to say that our commercial life could be maintained in vigorous health with any other than the world's monetary standard, is like saying that our physical and material well-being could be preserved if we could and did shut out the beneficent light and heat of the sun of the universe. International commerce is part of our existence. We cannot live without it, as our farmer, who is our principal exporter, ought to know. If we should try to, he and the man who lives by his personal services would be the first to discover what it means to be in the hands of the money-broker, as they found out before when we paid for our green-back debauch, and when Europe in 1893 began to doubt our intentions as to silver.

The quality of the money and currency which we need being established, the question is as to its quantity. I have endeavored to show that this quantity is dependent on the demands of business. The amount of money in circulation is the amount needed to carry on the trade and commerce of the country, and that ought to fix the amount of money in existence. A currency that responds to the demands of business, expanding with a brisk trade and a large demand for the tool of exchange, and contracting when trade is dull and the demand is light, is an elastic currency. Our own currency is not elastic. No human prescience, least of all the prescience of the excellent but inexperienced gentlemen who are elected to Congress, can fix the amount of money that is needed by the business interests of this country. They have attempted it and failed. They have not understood the great truth which was illustrated in the imaginary account of the transactions between the storekeeper and the wheat buyer and the wheat buyer and the farmer, the fact that one dollar of money or currency carries many dollars of transactions. They have added to the currency of the country since 1873 the sum of $1,657,000,000, but the business of the country has employed only $937,000,000 of this great amount. Was there ever a finer demonstration of folly? And this enormous and needless addition to the money of the country has been expensive. Without counting other elements of extravagance, the government has lost $156,000,000 on the value of the bullion it purchased under the acts of 1878 and 1890 alone. -Business alone can determine how much money a country needs, and business has determined in this country that politicians have added too much to our stock of money, and that they have wasted valuable time, energy, and wealth in the commission of this grievous mistake.

Not only has the country a great supply of money. It has too much of certain kinds, and no elastic currency whatever. It has more than it ever had before, and more than is held by any great commercial nation. Moreover, we have enough gold to sustain a bank-note or paper circulation, on the basis of the Treasury's gold reserve, greater than our whole present circulation.

There is no need for more money in this country. There is every reason why the present gold standard should be maintained. I do not believe in international bimetallism, but, even if its adoption would be beneficial to the world, the question is now wholly speculative. Until there is a stronger movement towards that end than now exists, this country has only one of two courses to take—either to retain its present system, which makes the gold dollar the standard, or to adopt the South American system, which makes the silver dollar the standard. Most of the present talk about international bimetallism comes from politicians who are trying to deceive the people, and especially the silver men. They are fishing for silver votes. But what the silver men want is the free coinage of silver at the ratio of 16 to 1, and they want this country to adopt that system independently of other nations. They do not care what happens to the commerce of the country, nor to the farmer, whose products constitute the larger part of the goods that are sold to foreign countries, so long as they can sell fifty cents worth of silver for a dollar. The international bimetallic politician cannot deceive the silver-mine owner, nor can the silver-mine owner, I trust, deceive the farmer, the mechanic, the wage-earner, the professional man, the

THE DEAD-HORSE PARTY THINKS IT IS DOING ALL THE WORK

merchant, who make up the people for whose benefit this country ought to be governed.

In the course of these papers, while I have been
trying to establish the propositions that the money
we need is honest money, the world's money, and,
under existing conditions, gold money; that the
amount we need cannot be determined by politicians,
but must be fixed by the demands of business; and
that these demands have shown that we already possess more money than we need, and that the redun-
dance has cost us dear, I have also shown that prices
are not dependent on money, that the so-called "demonetization" of silver did not cause a fall in prices,
and that the country has prospered greatly since
1873, notwithstanding the mournful outcries of the
bimetallists. Whatever may be the present state of
the public mind in this country on the subject of
money, I have no doubt that reflection and study
will bring the people to the conclusions that I have
reached. There is no economic problem, especially
no problem involving a moral issue, that the people
of the United States have not solved on the side of
honesty and common-sense, after a full and free discussion. Such a free and full discussion is now in
progress on the money question, and I am confident
that the United States will not consent to become
one of the cheap-money nations of the earth, but
will insist on remaining among the sound-money
nations.

BIMETALLISM IN HISTORY

" *Now these are the names of the different pieces of their gold, and of their silver, according to their value. And the names are given by the Nephites : for they did not reckon after the manner of the Jews who were at Jerusalem ; neither did they measure after the manner of the Jews, but they altered their reckoning and their measure, according to the minds and the circumstances of the people, in every generation, until the reign of the Judges ; they having been established by King Mosiah.*"—BOOK OF MORMON, BOOK OF ALMA, chapter viii., verse 8.

The only supernatural authority which has been found for the almost universal practice of trying to make two unequal things equal is that which is printed above from the Book of Mormon. The authority must stand on its merits. The fact, however, of the failure of the efforts to use silver and gold as the standard of value, as if their equality could be compelled, leaves this solitary utterance of alleged inspiration in a bad way.

WHEN the Puritans came to Massachusetts Bay in 1630, England alone of all the nations of Europe was endeavoring to maintain the double standard. On the Continent of Europe silver was frankly the standard. That great commercial country, Holland, maintained the silver standard from 1609 until recent years.

When this country was discovered the store of gold and silver in the world was very small. The quantity of the product from 1493 to 1850 was 8 of silver to 1 of gold, but the ratio of value was 10.75 of silver to 1 of gold. This difference may be accounted for by the greater comparative difficulty of obtaining gold. At this period gold came from West Africa, while silver was mined in Saxony and Bohemia. The relative values of the two metals have changed with the relative products of the mines. At the same time, the use of silver as money, which is as old as the coinage of the precious metals, shows that there are other causes than varying production that govern the price of the white metal, and when we come to the era of demonetization of silver we shall find the most potent of all causes, except, perhaps the discovery of the great silver mines of the West.

In 1630 when the Puritans came to Massachusetts, and when the commercial Hollanders were in New Amsterdam, the world's supply of the two metals was still very small. During this period gold had been found in New Granada, silver mines that had been worked by the Aztecs had been discovered by the Spaniards in Mexico, the still celebrated mines of Potosi, in Bolivia, had been found, and the patio process of working ore had been invented. Between 1601 and 1620 more than three times as much silver was produced as had been mined up to 1545, and its price had fallen until 12.25 ounces of silver were required for the purchase of an ounce of gold. In the next twenty years there was a slight decline of product, but the output of both gold and silver was still very large, while the price of silver fell so that the ratio between it and gold was 14 to 1. Here was a relative decrease in the product of silver, accompanied by an important fall in price.

In the meantime England was struggling with bimetallic difficulties in its attempt to sustain the two metals. Gold was rising in value when James I. came to the throne, and during the period which we are now considering—1600 to 1792—gold rose or silver fell until the ratio between the two increased from 11.80 to 15.17. In the intervening years it had not been less than 12.25, but several

times it had been higher than 15.17. An attempt
was made in this reign to fix the ratio by law at
13 to 1 at a time when the market ratio was really
about 12 to 1, and the consequence was the exportation of silver from the kingdom and general distress
among the working-people. In 1614 the king or-
dered that the exportation of coin should cease.
This was naturally ineffective. Proclamation after
proclamation followed, and Charles I. continued the
absurd financial policy of his father. The Star
Chamber undertook the enforcement of the proc-
lamations, and in 1636 there was a further demonstration of Gresham's law. The guineas were
selling for a premium in clipped shillings, and the
law undertook to fix their value, decreeing that a
guinea should not be taken for more than a certain
number of shillings. The good shillings were worth
more than this and at once disappeared in the melting-pot, the worn and clipped shillings alone appear-
ing in circulation. Trade sprang up in the good
shillings, and in the case before the Star Chamber
seven persons were convicted of "culling out the
most weighty pieces of the coin of this realm and
melting them down and exporting the same, as well
as foreign coin and bullion, to foreign ports." The
culprits were fined £8100, it having been shown to
the satisfaction of the Star Chamber that they had
made a profit of between £7000 and £8000 a year
by their practices,

In the reigns of William III. and George I. various efforts were made to stop the traffic in gold and good silver coin. French louis-d'or and moidores were found circulating in England at a valuation greater than their intrinsic worth. The law, therefore, decreed that they should pass for their real worth, and they immediately disappeared from circulation. Under an act of William III. (1696), which endured for sixteen days, the guinea was made worth twenty-six shillings. At the end of that brief time another act made the guinea worth twenty-two shillings. Both were ineffectual.·

Nothing but clipped or cheap money passed. Gold was undervalued as to worn shillings, and overvalued as to good shillings, while the good shillings were melted into bullion and bought and sold as a commodity. In 1699 the silver of the kingdom was recoined at an enormous loss to the Government, and at about the same time John Locke came to the conclusion, which he stated in a letter to Sir John Somers, Keeper of the Great Seal, that there should be only one metal coined, and that should be silver, for, notwithstanding the theoretical double standard of Great Britain, silver was " the money of the world," as Locke stated it to be, just as much in the time of William III. and George I. as it had been in the days when the patriarchs of the Old Testament bought their fields and flocks with silver shekels.

Notwithstanding the recoinage, clipped silver continued to circulate and the new and good coins disappeared. In the last forty years of the seventeenth century only £64,000 was brought to the mint to be coined. The speculative character of the currency brought great distress. In 1717 Sir Isaac Newton, then Master of the Mint, was asked by George I. for an opinion, and he recommended the reduction of the guinea to twenty-one shillings. This did not retain the good silver, for then the guinea was worth only 20s. 8d.

In the meantime the currency difficulties of the mother country were experienced in the American colonies, where, in 1652, a mint had been illegally established at Boston for the coinage of light "Pine-tree" shillings. Finally the evil became so great that, in 1774, an act of Parliament was passed limiting the right to coin silver to the Government and making it a legal tender by tale to the amount of £25. Above that it was legal tender by weight only.

This was the state of the silver question when the first coinage act of this country was passed in 1792. The act of 1774 was powerless to fix the mutual ratio of gold and silver values. The ratio in 1773 and 1774 was 14.62 to 1. In 1775 it rose to 14.72, but in 1776, when the act was extended, for at first it was only temporary, the ratio fell to 14.55, and in 1777 it fell still further, to 14.54. Silver grew dearer, notwithstanding adverse legislation in Great Britain.

II

A SINGLE STANDARD ADOPTED IN EUROPE

THE first coinage act for the United States was passed in 1792. Silver was actually first coined in 1794, and gold in 1795. The first silver dollar contained the same number of grains of fine silver as the standard dollar of to-day. Gold was coined in 1795, and the gold dollar contained 24.75 grains of pure gold.

England was still struggling with the currency question. Her commerce, manufactures, and working-people were suffering by reason of uncertainty as to the value of her circulating coins. Although the gold sovereign was the standard of value, silver was a legal tender for all debts. It is true that it was a legal tender by tale only to the amount of £25, but for amounts above that it was legal tender by weight. In the early part of the eighteenth century silver was generally supposed in commercial circles to be the English standard, and Adam Smith, in his explanation of the principle of foreign exchange, assumed that the metallic currencies of England and France were the same, and that both were silver. In this country we began by undervaluing gold, making the ratio 15 to 1, whereas the true ratio, in 1792, was 15.17 to 1. The latter was the ratio in England.

England adopted the single gold standard in 1798, six years after the enactment of our first coinage law. The temporary law of 1774 having been continued in 1776, was again extended in 1798 by acts which prohibited the importation of light silver coin, restrained the tender thereof beyond a certain sum, suspended the coinage of silver, and prohibited the reception of any silver to be coined, or any silver already coined to be delivered. The first of the acts of 1798 ran by its terms to January 1, 1799, and in that year the two coinage and currency acts of 1798 were revived and made perpetual.

Thus England passed under the gold standard; for gold becomes the single standard of a country when the mints are closed to private coinage of other metals. The silver that was in circulation continued to pass from hand to hand at the established rate of 21 to the guinea, much to its advantage, for the suspension of further coinage of silver bullion raised the value of both the gold and the current silver coins. Silver was overrated by the mint laws, for while its market price was ranging from 5s. an ounce to 5s. 1½d., it would have become worth 5s. 2d. by being coined.

The effect of the act of 1798 on the comparative prices of silver and gold was not serious. Silver

rose from 5s. 4d. to 5s. 6d. under the act of 1797,
restricting the payment of specie by the Bank of
England in anticipation of a possible discount on
bank-notes, but in September of the same year it fell
back to 5s. 1d., and it remained in that neighborhood for some time. The following are the ratios of
values for the ten years following the passage of the
act of 1798:

1799	15.74 to 1	1804	15.41 to 1
1800	15.68 to 1	1805	15.79 to 1
1801	15.46 to 1	1806	15.52 to 1
1802	15.26 to 1	1807	15.43 to 1
1803	15.41 to 1	1808	16.08 to 1

From this statement, taken from Dr. Soetbeer's
tables, it appears that the market value of silver
during the five years following 1799 was higher
than the price obtaining that year. In 1803 France
adopted by law the silver franc as the monetary unit,
and Belgium, Italy, Greece, and Switzerland followed.
These nations then fixed the ratio at 15½ to 1.
The product of silver between 1801–1810 was a
little more than 50 per cent. of the total product of
the two metals, and while the price decreased in
1805, probably in consequence of the increased output, it increased in 1806 and 1807, presumably in consequence of the acts of the Continental Governments.
In 1808 the price fell to a point lower than it had
ever yet reached, but it recovered in 1809, 1810, and
1811, although it did not reach the prices of 1801
and the year immediately following.

The gold standard was not formally adopted by England until .1816, and even that act was followed by a general rise in the price of silver. Gold seems to have been chosen instead of silver, because the "common people" had found it more convenient. Transactions of any importance required so great a weight of silver that the burden of transportation became onerous and expensive. Native gold coins were not circulating in England in the last years of the seventeenth century, but the French gold, undervalued at home, as we have already seen, was circulating at more than its intrinsic worth. Lord Liverpool, speaking of this era, said :

"It is evident that * * * the common people had become accustomed to the use of gold coins, and the reason which induced them still to prefer them was, perhaps, the convenience of making large payments in coins of that metal."

Silver is still legal tender in Great Britain, but only to the amount of £2, and the legal ratio is 14.28781 to 1. Silver is coined on account of the Government only. Gold is coined at private account at the fixed rate of £3 17s. 10½d. per ounce. Practically the Bank of England alone sends gold bars to the mint for coinage, paying individual owners of bullion £3 17s. 9d., the 1½d. being supposed to compensate the bank for the loss of interest while the bars are being transformed into coin. Most of the English colonies have adopted the gold stand-

ard and the monetary system of the mother country.
The monetary unit in Canada, however, is the gold
dollar of the United States. The Straits Settlements
and Hong-Kong have adopted the single silver standard, because it is in harmony with the currency of
the adjoining peoples.

The British India currency law dates back to 1835.
It makes the country silver monometallic, and the
rupee the monetary unit. The mohur is a gold coin,
but gold is not a legal tender. The ratio of coinage
is 15 to 1. The recent suspension of silver coinage
for private account places India on a gold basis, and
unless there is a return to the old order the gold
standard must be formally adopted. A money standard of a metal that cannot be coined on private account is an anomaly that will not endure.

It will be seen from an examination of the various
coinage laws of Europe that Locke's dictum was
growing in favor, and that the experiences of the
commercial countries of the world had gradually led
men of affairs to the conclusion that no nation could
maintain a double standard. The growth of international commerce had led to the invention of bills
of exchange. The rate for bills of exchange was
easily computed if the countries between which they
circulated possessed the same standard of value, the
same ratio, and coins of like intrinsic value ; but as
this was never the case, and the price varied with
fluctuations in the market values of the two metals,

with their exports and imports, with legislative acts, and with increase or diminution of product, the trade in bills of exchange became a speculation in gold, and silver. Foreign commerce and domestic trade became unsettled. Therefore, at the beginning of the present century there was a general tendency in Europe towards monometallism. England chose gold and France silver. But although it was the intention of the French to establish a single silver standard, the law of 1803 was bimetallic, and gold was not driven out of circulation until under the Napoleonic wars the price of gold rose, and silver alone circulated. From 1820 to 1847 gold was constantly at a premium in France.

When England adopted the single gold standard the Netherlands was a silver monometallic country, but, while it did not follow England's example, it adopted the double standard in 1816, returning in 1847 to the single silver standard.

Germany was a single silver standard country until its currency reform of 1871. Austria has also been a single silver standard country, although it is now putting into operation the single gold standard system.

III

THE GOLD MOVEMENT IN EUROPE

THE tendency of European countries in the early part of the present century was towards the adoption of the single standard. This course was dictated by common prudence and a desire to simplify transactions between the various countries.

M. Chevalier was the most conspicuous advocate in Europe of the use of silver as a money metal, and he is authority for the statement that gold disappeared from France during the Napoleonic wars and was not in circulation, while Mr. Giffen, the eminent English statistician, asserts that gold was constantly at a premium in France from 1820 to 1850. During the thirty years France was a silver country and gold was expelled, until in 1848, the Bank of France had hardly any gold in its vaults. It ought to be explained that it is a mistake to suppose that the French law of 1803 first fixed the ratio of 15½ to 1. If there is any magic in that ratio to keep the metals at a parity, it had an opportunity to show itself in the reign of Louis XVI., for Colonne fixed the ratio 15½ to 1 in 1785, and the statute of 1803 merely affirmed what already existed, and extended its life.

Colonne chose the ratio because gold was thereby overvalued.

In 1785 the commercial ratio was 14.92 to 1, and in 1803 it was 15.41. This ratio was maintained for two years, but in 1805 it became 15.79 to 1; in 1806 it was 15.52; in 1807 it fell below the French legal ratio once more, but gold recovered, and in 1808 the actual ratio was 16.08 to 1. It was not again as low as $15\frac{1}{2}$ until 1814, and for six years gold was overvalued by the French coinage law. In 1820, however, the ratio was once more above $15\frac{1}{2}$, and remained above for thirty years. It did not fall again until 1851, under the influence of the gold discoveries in California and Australia. Once more the ratio was below $15\frac{1}{2}$ for one year only. In 1852 it was 15.59. It again fell below $15\frac{1}{2}$ in 1853, and remained below for eight years. In 1861 the actual and legal ratios in France were the same; for the next five years gold was overvalued. In 1867 it was again undervalued, and the difference since then has been increasing, owing to the depreciation of silver.

The experience of France in undertaking to maintain the parity of the two metals was not happy. Since Colonne determined on the ratio of $15\frac{1}{2}$ to 1, one hundred and ten years ago, that ratio has been below the market ratio seventy-three years; it has been equal to the market ratio one year, and above it thirty-six years. In other words, it has expressed the truth once during that long period. Since 1803 gold has been undervalued in France sixty-eight years, correctly valued one year, and overvalued twenty-two years.

It was the intention of the framers of the law of 1803 to provide France with a single standard of silver, but nature was against them, and by circulating gold the tendency was to exclude their favorite metal from circulation, until war came to the assistance of the financiers, when the ratio of $15\frac{1}{2}$ to 1 became an undervaluation of gold, whereupon gold disappeared and silver constituted the circulation.

Silver was the circulating medium in 1803, and remained so until the great gold discoveries brought a flood of the yellow metal to Europe. Between 1851 and 1853 gold began to appear in the French circulation, and the people, like the people of England in the last decade of the seventeenth century, found it preferable, by reason of its smaller bulk and weight, to the heavy five-franc pieces.

This state of things lasted until 1867, when the discovery of the great silver deposits had begun to be made. The Comstock lode was discovered in 1859, but the Belcher Bonanza was not found until 1864; the Chollar-Potosi bonanza in 1865; the Hale and Norcross bonanza in 1866. During the period when the gold discoveries were being made the price of silver gradually rose in London from $59\frac{1}{4}d.$ per ounce in 1848 to $61\frac{3}{8}d.$ in 1864, but it did not fall

below 60d. until 1873, when the average price was
59$\frac{1}{4}d$.

In the meantime the commercial countries of Europe were coming to the gold standard. The attempt to maintain the single silver standard was about to be abandoned. So much silver was deposited for coinage at the mint of France that the mint could not have performed its expected task in much less than two years. The currency was becoming inflated. Exchanges were disturbed, and France was suffering from cheap money. In addition to the silver thrown upon the market by the extraordinary increase of the output of the silver mines of this country, the closing of the German mints to the coinage of silver and the sale of the Government's stores for the purchase of gold needed for the adoption of the gold standard had reduced the price of silver.

Germany abandoned silver in 1871 and adopted the single gold standard. The suspension of silver coinage was followed by the melting down of the old coins and the sale of the bullion. This sale was stopped in 1879. While it was going on the price of silver in London fell from 60$\frac{1}{2}d$. in 1871 to 51$\frac{1}{4}d$. in 1879. It is undoubtedly true that Germany's demonetization of silver had much to do with this decline in price; but, as has been already shown, a decline had set in six years before 1871.

During that six years silver had gone down only about 1d. on the ounce. While, therefore, the whole

7

decline in price from 1871 to 1879 cannot be charged
to the action of Germany, most of it is evidently due
to the coinage law of the new empire. Since Germany stopped selling, the price of silver has declined
more than 20*d.*, and this decline has not been ar-
rested by the two silver purchase laws enacted by
the United States.

It is fair to assume that the decline has been partly
aided by the closing of the mints of the Latin Union
to silver, and by the action of the Austrian Government in deciding to adopt the single gold standard.
The Latin Union was formed in 1865. The metallic
coinage of Continental Europe was in a most deplor-
able condition, and the silver countries found themselves, in contrast with Great Britain, at a serious
commercial disadvantage. Therefore, France, Belgium, and Switzerland formed a union, and they were
subsequently joined by Greece and Italy. Silver
token coinage was adopted, and, following the English system, it was made legal tender to the amount
of 50 francs, equivalent to £2, or $10.

In 1876 the mints of the Latin Union were closed
to the coinage of silver on private account, and while,
as had been said, it is fair to assume that this action
had some effect on the price of silver, that effect was
not great, for the price was 52¾*d.* in 1876, and it was
not until 1881 that it fell permanently below 52*d.*
Spain adopted the monetary system of the Latin
Union in 1868, but in 1878 determined that silver

should be coined on state account only. Austria
suspended silver coinage in 1879.

While the fall in the price of silver was inducing
the United States to "rehabilitate" that metal by the
Allison Purchase Act, Europe was adopting the single
gold standard.

IV

IN THE UNITED STATES BEFORE 1873

THE experience of the Government of the United States with bimetallism during the first eighty years of its history was somewhat similar to that of France. It had a theoretical double standard, but was practically monometallic. Its monetary history was also like that of England in the latter part of the seventeenth century. Its good coin was hoarded and sold abroad, and the coin that circulated was the worn and light foreign coin that came into a country where it was able to procure more than its intrinsic worth.

The first coinage act of this country was passed in 1792. The question of currency at that time seems to have excited merely a languid interest in Congress, and for some time it was doubtful if a mint would be established. The probable cost of its maintenance seemed to be an insuperable objection. The matter of coinage was practically settled by the executive branch of the Government. For once those old and persistent political enemies, Hamilton and Jefferson, came together and decided that both metals should be used, and that the ratio should be 15 to 1.

It was the English ratio and the French system

coming together. England was examining the coinage question for herself, and had temporarily suspended free coinage of silver, but the people of this country had little commercial experience to instruct them in the consequences of bimetallism, and accepted the double standard because gold and silver had both been the money metals of the world from time immemorial. After a fashion that has not yet gone out of date the people of this country insisted on acquiring their experience for themselves and paying for it.

1792–1834 SILVER MONOMETALLISM UNDER DOUBLE STANDARD

THE coinage act was passed in 1792, but the first silver was actually coined in 1794 and the first gold in 1795. Under the first statute the silver dollar weighed 416 grains, 1485 parts pure and 179 parts alloy. The fine silver in a dollar was, therefore, then as now, 371.25 grains. The gold eagle weighed 270 grains, $\frac{11}{12}$ fine, so that a gold dollar contained 24.75 grains of fine gold. The ratio established was not the true ratio. Gold was undervalued. An ounce of gold was worth more than 15 ounces of silver; it was worth 15.17 ounces. The new coins, as has been pointed out, did not circulate. The Government itself was largely responsible, for it permitted cheap and worn foreign coin which came to it in payment

of its customs dues to go out into the circulation,
once more, to illustrate the truth of Gresham's law.
Gold was exported, and quantities of our new eagles
were seen in the show-windows of European gold-
smiths. In 1793 only were the legal and market ratios the same. In 1794 the ratio was 15.37 to 1, and
not once so long as the ratio of 15 to 1 prevailed, except in 1793, was gold down to the value fixed by
Congress.

Neither the gold nor the silver circulating, the coinage of silver dollars was suspended in 1806, and none
were coined again until 1836, when 1000 were struck
off. None were coined after that until 300 were
struck off in 1839. Then the coinage went on, but
it was 1869 before the number minted in any year
reached 400,000, and 1871 before it was 1,000,000.
In 1873, the year when silver was demonetized, the
mints coined only $293,600, which measures the de-
sire of the bullion owners of that time for the pres-
ervation of silver as a money metal at the ratio of
16 to 1 then prevailing.

Gold entirely disappeared from circulation by 1817,
and no gold dollars whatever were coined until 1849,
after the discovery of gold in California. The estab-
lishment of American coins as circulating currency
was a work of great labor, attended with many difficulties. The early years of the Republic were years
of struggle war, and financial distress. After the
dissolution of the United States Bank the business

of the country was carried on by means of paper currency of more than uncertain value. Specie payments were suspended in 1814 by all the banks except those of New England, and metallic money was practically unknown.

So disastrous to the material interests of the country was the lack of confidence in the paper currency that in 1816 the money question came up in Congress for discussion. The United States Bank was rechartered, and the right of establishing branches with the privilege of issue was granted to it. After that for a time the country had paper money based upon foreign coin.

Several efforts were made to establish our own coin and to prevent the inroad of foreign coin, but nature insisted on having its own way. A proposition was made to Congress to return to the devices that had been found futile in the reigns of James I. and Charles I., and to prohibit the exportation of specie. In 1816 and 1819 laws were passed providing that foreign gold coin should not be legal tender in this country, but this accomplished nothing, and in 1823 all foreign gold coins were made receivable for the public lands, while in 1834 an act was passed making the dollars of Mexico, Peru, Chili, and Central America, and the five-franc piece of France, legal tender at their nominal value, when of full weight.

1834–73 GOLD MONOMETALLISM UNDER DOUBLE STANDARD

In 1834, foreign gold not being legal tender under the laws of 1816 and 1819, the basis of our circulation was foreign silver and fractional coin. A movement now began in the interest of gold. Like the silver movement of to-day, it was largely protective. The gold mines of North Carolina, discovered in 1801, had begun to yield a generous output in 1828. About the same time gold was discovered in Georgia, and great results were expected. Congress undertook to care for the American gold interest by changing the ratio and by also changing the composition of the gold coin. The ratio was changed from 15 to 1 to 16 to 1. The weight of the silver dollar was changed from 416 to 412.5 grains, but the fine silver in the coin, 371.25 grains, remained unchanged. The fine gold in a dollar of the other metal, however, was reduced from 24.75 to 23.22.

Thus, in the interest of an American industry, the gold dollar, which had been worth under the old law $1.038, became worth 97½ cents. Silver became the more valuable metal and disappeared from the circulation. Up to the passage of this law about $12,000,-000 of gold had been coined in this country, chiefly in half-eagles. Eagles had not been coined since 1804, and their coinage was not resumed until 1838. Double eagles were not coined until 1850, at the time when the recent gold discoveries had greatly increased the production of the metal. In 1849 an act was passed providing that the gold dollar should contain 25.8 grains of fine gold.

No sooner had the silver dollar been underrated than silver coins began to be exported from this country in large quantities. Silver coin became scarce in the circulation, except the Spanish-American coins with which every one was familiar thirty years ago. So greatly was the market value of silver in excess of its coinage value that the fractional coins began to disappear, and in 1853 our fractional silver was made subsidiary and token money by the reduction of the amount of fine silver in the coins. It was at the same time made legal tender to the value of $5.

Thus the country continued under a practical 'gold monometallism, with subsidiary or token silver coins, until the passage of the act of 1873. The silver dollar was not in circulation, because it was too valuable for that use at the existing ratio. It had never been in circulation. The only silver dollars with which the people of this country were familiar were those of the South American and Central American countries mentioned in the act of 1834.

The act of 1834 may be said to have deliberately driven silver out of circulation and out of use as money, except for small change, because gold was overvalued for that purpose. And yet the price of silver was not affected by that action of the United States, as the following quotations from the London market reports will show :

1833	$59\frac{3}{16}d.$	1838	$59\frac{1}{2}d.$
1834	$59\frac{15}{16}d.$	1839	$60\frac{2}{3}d.$
1335	$59\frac{11}{16}d.$	1840	$60\frac{3}{8}d.$
1836	$60d.$	1841	$60\frac{1}{16}d.$
1837	$59\frac{9}{16}d.$	1842	$59\frac{7}{16}d.$

Silver increased in price, and the increase continued during the years when the output of gold was growing by reason of the discoveries of gold mines in California and Australia. But silver began to fall, as has already been shown, after 1866. In 1873, however, the law that was passed omitting the silver dollar from the coinage merely made statutory a fact that had existed for nearly forty years.

V

WHEN the act of 1873 was passed extraordinary movements affecting currency were going on everywhere. That act has been made altogether too important in the discussion of bimetallism. It was in reality a mere formal declaration of a fact. Silver was not demonetized by it. That was done by the act of 1834, changing the ratio of the two metals and the amount of fine gold in a dollar. The act of 1853, reducing the amount of silver in the fractional currency and making it token money, was also a movement strengthening gold monometallism. Not only was the single gold standard the result of the two laws, it was the declared intention of their movers and advocates to adopt the gold standard in this manner. The silver dollar was not in circulation, because it was worth $1.04 in gold, and no one made an effort, as by urging a revision of the legal ratio, to make it agree with the market ratio, to secure its restoration. The great fall in silver that was to occur shortly had not set in. Therefore when the bill, accompanied by the reports of the Secretary of the Treasury and Mr. John J. Knox, its author, was pre-

sented to Congress no comment was made on the
fact that the 412½ grain dollar was dropped by it
from the silver coinage of the country. The bill
simply provided that certain pieces, naming them,
should constitute the silver coinage of the United
States. The 412½ grain dollar was not included.
The trade dollar was authorized, and, by mistake,
a legal-tender quality up to $5 was bestowed upon
it as upon the subsidiary coins. Subsequently the
mistake was rectified. Really, the trade dollar was
not part of the coinage of the country. It was simply a bit of silver weighing 420 grains, stamped by
the Government at the expense of the owner of the
bullion, to be sold at a profit in Oriental countries.

It has been the fashion of some controversialists
to say that the silver dollar was surreptitiously demonetized. History does not sustain the contention.
As has been seen from a simple record of the events,
silver was demonetized in 1834. But whether the
method of passing the act of 1873 was or was not
surreptitious has no bearing on the merits of bimetallism or of monometallism. They must stand
on a sounder basis than that or fall altogether. As
a matter of fact the bill was before Congress for
nearly three years. It was first submitted to the
Senate on April 25, 1870, and to the House on June
25. It was debated in the Senate and passed on
June 10, 1871, by a vote of 36 to 14. It was debated in the House in 1872 and passed, with amend-

ments, by a vote of 110 to 13. It was passed in the Senate, as amended, January 17, 1873, a conference committee was appointed, and the bill became a law, February 12, 1873. The reports accompanying the bill, especially Mr. Knox's, explained the fact, and the purpose of dropping the silver dollar from the coinage. This fact was therefore brought home to the members, who discussed it, and Mr. William D. Kelley, Chairman of the Committee on Coinage, Weights and Measures, in reporting the bill to the House, said that it had been most carefully and deliberately considered by the committee, who had gone over it "line by line and word by word." Although he subsequently joined the advocates of free coinage, he said on this occasion that "it is impossible to retain the double standard."

All this is interesting as history, but it has nothing to do with the merits of the question. After 1873 and until 1878 the country was not only in fact but in law on a gold basis. Silver had begun to be cheaper, as has already been shown; but it was not until 1876 that the fall had become great enough to arouse the owners of mines and the friends of silver generally to the beginning of a contest.

By 1876 the price of silver in the London market had dropped from $59\frac{1}{4}d$. an ounce in 1873 to $52\frac{3}{4}d$. The causes of this decline open up a very interesting field of investigation and discussion. The demand for gold had been growing since 1849. The production of this metal in twenty-five years from 1851 to 1875 was enormous. The value of the output during that period was $3,317,625,000 as against a silver product of $1,395,125,000. Prof. Laughlin, in his " History of Bimetallism in the United States," has shown that this output of gold was a trifle more than the gold product of the 357 years from 1493 to 1850. The price of gold fell, and consequently obtained a still wider circulation as money. It drove silver into the melting-pot, and threatened the small change not only of the United States but of Continental Europe. There the Latin Union was formed and the franc was lightened just as our own 50, 25, and 10 cent pieces were lightened. In 1840 the annual production of gold was about $15,000,000, in 1851 it was $150,000,000. Between 1852 and 1864 . France absorbed $680,000,000 of gold and sent abroad $345,000,000 of silver. There was no disposition manifested anywhere to surrender gold and to procure silver in its place. On the contrary, a decided preference was shown for gold, and nowhere more than in France, where, as time went on, silver coins were changed and limited in purchasing power, but gold was left untouched.

In this country the annual product of gold increased from $889,085 in 1847 to $10,000,000 in 1848. The next year it was $40,000,000, the next $50,000,000, and from then to 1859 it ranged from $50,000,000 to $65,000,000. In 1858 the product of silver in the United States was $500,000. Before then it had never exceeded $50,000 in a year. It was not until after 1860 that it reached $2,000,000 a year. From that year it rapidly increased, and in 1873 it was $35,750,000, while the product of gold for the same period was $36,000,000. The production of silver increased, and gold about held its own.

Undoubtedly this increase in the supply of silver made the metal cheaper, but there were other causes than the increase of supply to cheapen silver. Alongside with the increase there was a decrease of demand. From 1848 to 1860, when the annual product of gold in this country was increasing from $10,000,000 to $50,000,000, $60,000,000 and $65,-000,000, the product of silver was inconsiderable.

But the price of silver did not materially fall, notwithstanding the increased production of the years immediately following 1860. The highest prices ranged from $60\frac{3}{4}d$. to $61.16d$. But in 1873 the price of silver fell so much that the average price was $59\frac{1}{4}d$., and in the three following years the fall was so great that the lowest price in London in 1876 was $46\frac{3}{4}d$. and the highest $58\frac{1}{2}d$. By this time the annual product of silver had grown to be $91,208,750 as against $115,756,750 of gold. The interpretation of this is at least that the fall in price did not result wholly from the increase of supply. The demand had a good deal to do with it. Much stress is laid on the new German coinage act and the

consequent increase of the supply of silver in the
world's bullion market. The fact is that from 1871
to 1876 the German sales of silver did not exceed
$30,000,000. At the same time the German demand
for gold for the purpose of establishing the single
gold standard was about $414,000,000. This de-
mand for gold had a greater effect on the price of
silver than the sale of the silver coins for bullion.
At the same time there was a decreased demand for
silver on the Continent. Belgium and Holland had
already closed their mints to silver, and the French
mint was closed in 1876. India, too, helped the
depreciation of the price of silver. Her indebtedness to England temporarily suspended her enormous power for absorbing silver. In 1869-70 the
excess of India imports of silver was $36,601,685;
in 1870-71 it fell to $4,709,685; in 1872-73 it
was down to $3,523,220. It was not back to large
figures until 1878. The effect of the decreased demand is shown in our own statistics of exports. In
1871 our total exports of silver amounted to $31,-
755,780; in 1876 they were down to $25,329,252,
notwithstanding the greatly increased production,
which in the same year advanced from $23,000,000
to $38,800,000. Nor did the decline of exportations
cease with 1876. In 1882 they were only $16,829,-
599, while the silver product of the country had
grown to be $46,800,000.

In addition to the increased supply and the exceptional state of things in India, the fact that silver had generally gone out of use as a standard of value in Europe must be taken into consideration in seeking for the reason of the fall in price in 1876. It was this fall that led to the movement in this country to " rehabilitate " silver. Before this, gold was the native product that appealed successfully to Congress for protection. Now silver was becoming the national metal. In 1876 Colorado was admitted as a State, the enabling act having been passed in 1875. The silver interests thus secured two Senators in Congress. In 1876 the products of gold and silver were about equal. By 1879 the annual product of silver exceeded in commercial value that of gold, and this excess steadily increased until 1893. There is no doubt, whatever may be said as to causes governing the market prior to 1876, that this rapid increase of silver production since then accounts in great measure for the great fall of price from an average of $52\frac{3}{4}d$. to about $33d$.

The movement for the free coinage of silver in 1876 was very brisk. Several bills were introduced in the House for the issue of coin notes and for the re-establishment of the silver dollar. One of these was passed, but received no consideration from the Senate. On November 5, 1877, Mr. Bland introduced a free coinage and unlimited legal-tender silver bill, which was passed, without debate and under suspension of the rules, by a vote of 163 to 34.

8

When the bill reached the Senate it was placed in charge of Mr. Allison, who reported it back from the Finance Committee with important amendments. The bill passed the Senate, February 15, 1878, by a vote of 48 to 21. As it passed it provided for the monthly purchase of not less than $2,000,000 worth of silver bullion or not more than $4,000,000 worth "at the market price thereof," the bullion to be coined into 412½ grain dollars. Silver certificates and an international monetary conference were provided for. Free coinage was defeated. After some protest the House concurred in the Senate amendments by a vote of 203 to 72. On February 28 President Hayes vetoed the bill. On the same day both houses passed it over his veto. While the discussion of these measures was in progress Senator Matthews secured the passage of a resolution declaring that the United States might lawfully redeem its bonds in silver dollars. The result of the passage of this resolution was immediately felt. Our bonds began to come back from Europe. In one week $10,000,000 of them were thrown upon the market, and the amount sent home was estimated by Mr. Allison to have reached $100,000,000. We had warning seventeen years ago of what actually resulted from the act of 1890.

Under the act of 1878 the Treasury never coined more than $2,000,000 worth of silver a month. Sometimes the bullion owners demanded more than

the market rates, when Secretary Sherman, inter-
preting the law as Mr. Carlisle has lately interpreted
it, declined to make the purchases. The Government found it almost impossible to force the new
silver dollars into circulation. The people would
not take them. The Clearing House in New York
declined to receive the certificates in settlement of
balances, until they were compelled to do so by an act
of Congress which forbade national banks from join-
ing an association governed by such a rule. The
Government did its best. It paid the cost of trans-
porting the dollars. It discontinued the issue of
legal-tender notes of denominations of less than five
dollars. It issued one, two, and five dollar silver certificates, and finally obtained a circulation for the
smaller of these.

Fortunately for the country, the surrender of large
amounts of national bank currency at this time made
a place for the new silver currency, so that all the
evil effects of a silver coinage adopted in the face of
the action of the commercial world and in antago-
nism to it were not felt. Under the act of 1878
the Government purchased 291,272,019 ounces of
silver, for which it paid $308,279,261. But out of
it the Government issued in coins 378,166,793 silver
dollars. The purchases of the Government did not
check the rapid decline in the price of silver, as is
shown by the following quotations of the average
London price per ounce :

1878	$52\frac{9}{16}d.$
1879	$51\frac{1}{4}d.$
1880	$52\frac{1}{4}d.$
1881	$51\frac{5}{8}d.$
1882	$51\frac{3}{8}d.$
1883	$50\frac{5}{8}d.$
1884	$50\frac{1}{4}d.$
1885	$48\frac{9}{16}d.$
1886	$45\frac{3}{8}d.$
1887	$44\frac{5}{8}d.$
1888	$42\frac{7}{8}d.$
1889	$42\frac{11}{16}d.$

The friends of silver were not satisfied. They insisted that the Government should do something more for their favorite metal. On June 17, 1890, the Senate passed a free coinage bill by a vote of 42 to 25. The House did not concur, and there was a compromise measure agreed upon by a conference committee, which became a law, known as the Sherman act. The law required the monthly purchase of 4,500,000 ounces, and the coinage every month of 2,000,000 ounces of the bullion so purchased until July 1, 1891. After that bars were to be coined for the redemption of the legal-tender Treasury notes authorized by the act, in the discretion of the Secretary. The act recited further that it was the "established policy of the United States to maintain the two metals on a parity with each other."

The Treasury purchased under the Sherman law 168,674,683 ounces at a cost $155,931,002. At 67 cents an ounce this bullion is worth $113,012,037, a loss to the Government of $42,918,965.

The operation of the Sherman law was quickly felt. Although there was no free coinage, Gresham's law began to act. Holders of American securities became alarmed lest they would be obliged to accept payment in silver, and a general hoarding and exportation of gold followed. The following table will show the increase of our exports of gold coin and gold bullion :

1888	$34,526,447
1889	50,933,460
1890	24,063,074
1891	79,086,581
1892	76,532,056
1893	79,775,820
Total	$344,917,438

Subtracting imports, there was in these years a net loss of gold to the United States of $230,234,403.

In the mean time the departure of gold was shown in another way. In January, 1890, of the customs dues received by the Government 92.6 per cent. were paid in gold; in December 88.3 per cent. was in gold. In December, 1891, the amount of gold received for customs dues had fallen to 65.4 per cent. ; in January, 1893, only 8.9 per cent. was paid in gold; and though the hoarded gold forced from the bank vaults by the currency famine of 1893 temporarily swelled the gold receipts from customs, the proportion in January, 1894, was but 17.6 per cent. ; from which it rapidly dwindled, until in October and November, 1894, gold receipts had entirely ceased.

The business distress which followed the loss of confidence in our securities, in one another, and in everything that usually commands the respect of business men, is only now beginning to depart, and it will return if the legislation of the new Congress is as foolish as that of its predecessors has been.

VI

CONGRESS was called together in the summer of 1893 for the purpose of repealing the Sherman act. After many vexatious delays, involving disaster and loss to the business interests of the country, a bill was passed unconditionally repealing the purchasing clause of the law. In the meantime, June 26, 1893, the Indian mints were closed to the free coinage of silver. While the effect on the monetary and commercial relations of India has not been what the authors of the act expected, the immediate result was a panic in silver. The price fell at once in London, reaching $30\frac{1}{2}d.$, the lowest point ever touched up to that date. This was in June. In July the price rose to $32\frac{1}{8}d.$, but in December it was down to $31\frac{1}{2}d.$ in London and 70.25 cents an ounce in New York. Silver is now (July 1, 1895) selling at $30\frac{4}{16}d.$ in London, and at $67\frac{1}{4}$ cents an ounce in New York, and in the meantime the production of gold has enormously increased. At the first of the year the price was down to $27\frac{7}{16}d.$ in London and $59\frac{3}{4}$ cents in New York, but since then the price of silver has risen with that of other commodities. In the calendar year of 1893 it was the largest known in the history of gold mining, the output being valued at $157,228,100. The gold output for 1894 was $181,-669,100, which was more than equal to the rate of gold and silver output of 1861–1865, and it is expected that the increase will continue indefinitely. In other words, the world will soon have as much gold as a basis of value as it had of both gold and silver together in the days before the act of 1873 was passed, before Germany was on a gold basis, and when the Latin Union was trying to keep the two unequal metals at parity.

VII

THESE developments raise the point as to whether the whole question of bimetallism, as compared with a single standard either of gold or silver, is not being satisfactorily answered by the course of events outside of legislation. Whatever may have been true in earlier periods, when governments were comparatively isolated, and practically omnipotent in influencing trade conditions within their respective boundaries, the developments of the last half - century—in breaking down international barriers, in the increasing dependence of governments upon the conditions of finance and commerce, in the unexampled development of international as compared with local affairs — have reached a point where laws are as powerless to affect the tides of commerce as are imaginary boundary - lines to limit the climates or change the natural relations of the territories through which they run. In other words, in the essential matters of currency, commerce has become all-powerful.

Fifty years ago the world's aggregate of coined money, silver and gold, was probably a fair supply

for commerce as it then existed. Since then the
question of supply and demand for coin currency
has been vitally affected by three factors, namely :

1. The development of facilities for communi-
cation, greater since 1840 than from the time of
Abraham to that date, and the corresponding developments of commercial expedients. These developments have reduced the absolute amount of
coin necessary for exchanges.

2. Discoveries of new deposits and cheapening
of gold and silver production in America, Australia,
and Africa. These have been so important in the
last half - century as to add to our supply of these
metals a greater amount than had been secured in a
thousand years before.

3. The increasing (now almost universal) extent
to which the use of silver as a basis for currency
has been renounced by one nation after another.

Of course it must be remembered that in the case
of a comparatively indestructible product, such as
gold or silver, the world's stock on hand is so great
as to permit its value to be affected but slowly by
any increase in the annual production. But, even
after all allowance has been made for this, during the
earlier part of the last half-century, while the first
and second of the suggested causes were in more
active operation than was the third, the actual result
was the inevitable one. The demand for gold and
silver decreased greatly when compared with their

rapidly increasing supply, and both were cheapened when compared with the price of labor.

During the last twenty-five years, however, the third factor has come so rapidly to the front that the civilized world (practically the whole world, so far as concerns commerical conditions) is now conducting its business upon the basis of gold alone.

The movement, which commenced in earnest as nearly as may be one hundred years ago, for the discarding of silver as a money metal, is now practically complete, having circled the commercial globe. Its incalculable force in tending steadily to depress the price of silver and appreciate that of gold is, therefore, practically spent; and we are relegated, as a basis for calculation as to the future, to the effect of the other causes noted, both of which are still in full operation. Commercial developements are still lessening the amount of metal required to facilitate a given quantity of exchanges; and the annual production of gold has of late so rapidly increased as to promise for the year 1895 a greater output of that metal alone than of both gold and silver combined during any four years before 1850. Indeed, the rate of increase of gold production during the last two years has been such that, if continued until 1900, it will have added, in gold alone, to our stock of precious metals, during this decade, more than the production of both silver and gold for any ten years previous to 1890.

124

It seems, therefore, clear, first, that the last quarter-century has been that in which has culminated a world-wide movement to displace silver and appreciate, comparatively, the commercial value of gold; that the operation of this cause is not merely practically at an end, but that its workings have coincided with and set in motion compensating forces; as a result of which the value of gold must henceforth steadily depreciate, as a consequence of the steadily increasing proportion which its supply from this time on will bear to the world's demand for its use.

THE END

www.ingramcontent.com/pod-product-compliance
Lightning Source LLC
Chambersburg PA
CBHW030600270326
41927CB00007B/991